Organisational Behaviour, Human Resource Management & Management

Organisational Behaviour, Human Resource Management & Management

Dr. Dileep Kumar M.
MA., MSW., (MHRM)., MPHILL., PHD., PGDBA, PGDHRM, PGDCA., DLL., DHA (UGC–NET)

SERIALS PUBLICATIONS
NEW DELHI (INDIA)

First Published - 2010

ISBN: 978-81-8387-315-4

Published by

SERIALS PUBLICATIONS
4830/24, Prahlad Street, Ansari Road
Darya Ganj, New Delhi-110002 (India)
Phone : 23245225 Fax : 91-11-23272135
E-mail: serials@satyam.net.in

This book is Dedicated
to my Mother

CONTENTS

PREFACE

A quality education is a custom design that addresses the unique abilities of each student and has a positive emotional experience. But present day education rarely integrate the practical exposure to students that enable them to develop operational understanding, especially subjects like business management. The business management courses are more of theory oriented than practice oriented. When the Harvard Business School was started, the faculty quickly realized that there were no textbooks suitable to a graduate program in business. In order to induce the managerial skills and operational understanding the business school faculty members have developed a method called case study method, with particular learning objectives in mind and are refined in the classroom before publication. The case studies consists of lot of information such as financial statements, time-lines, short biographies, collection of incidents, business volatility etc. Case studies are known for their contemporariness, concepts, broad understandings, referential data and the decision dilemmas which motivate a reader to be aware, analyze the complex issues and arrive at suitable inferences for effective decision making. Business case studies recount real life business situations that present to business executives a dilemma. Representing a broad range of management issues, this case study collection on OB, HR and General Management, provides faculty members, students, corporate trainers and management professionals with a variety of teaching and reference material. This book covers 25 case studies in Organizational Behaviour, Human Resource Management and

General Management arena that gives ample information on real life situations, incidents and issues in business area. I enjoyed going through this case study work book and I am quiet confident that it will be received well by faculty members, students, corporate trainers, and management professionals across global level.

Prof. Kiran Reddy
(CEO)
Acharya Institute of Management
Sciences (AIMS), Peenya, Bangalore.

Case 1

PLANNING, COORDINATION AND CONTROL

Sreeram Institute of Science and Technology, is one of the prestigious institutes in the field of Engineering and Applied Sciences, located in Kottayam, District Kerala. Within a period of 6 years it has secured 2nd best position of engineering college within the District. The management of SIST (Sreeram Institute of Science and Technology) decided to go for different professional programmes from 2006 onwards. They have decided to launch one MBA, a four semester residential programme, with four specializations like Finance, Marketing, Human Resource Management and Systems. They named it as Sreeram Institute of Management (SIM). The programme received adequate response from the local level and even from the entire state. Students from all over Kerala joined in MBA programme. The institute appointed 5 faculty members, Dean and an Administrator with Assistant Administrators to govern the institute initially.

Since the institute doesn't have a permanent building at the time of launch of the program, they started the course in a guesthouse-converted building with a syndicate room, a conference room, Dean's room, a faculty room, a general administration room and a classroom having the capacity of 60 students. The institute was well aware of the fact that they were running with limitations of infrastructure and facilities those compared to other business management schools in and around Kerala. In spite of limited infrastructure and facilities, the visibility and image secured already by the Sreeram College of Engineering (SCE), SIM (Sreeram Institute of Management) got around 50 students in the 2006 academic year. The management of SIM has strictly adhered to the quality of the students in the selection process and they restricted the admission to 50 seats against the total allotment of 60 seats.

The programme was launched from July 1st 2006. Since the students required better business and orientation, the Dean announced one week Student Personality Development programme from 1st July. The Dean of SIM has planned two day Personality Development and Attitude Building training module in the Hilly Valley Resort Kuttikkanam, located near Peerumedu Hills. The Dean of SIM realized the importance of Students Development Programme; especially to the Kerala students, who, in general, do not have high confidence on their communication skills. Since the Dean of the institute is from the field of Human Resource Management and he is well versed with the training and development programme. Being a visualiser and a trainer, he planned a 'Boot Camp' - Students Training Programme-with the support of an outside professional trainer and with the help of internal faculties.

In accordance with this some of the faculties in SIM had differences of opinion on conducting the training programme at Hilly Valley Resort Kuttikkanam. They were of the opinion that these modules can be run during the weekends within the campus with the available Engineering College Seminar Hall and the free ground. It would have provided better preparation and breathing space to the students who have come from distant places and different background. Further it reduces the expenditure on training programme. The activities incorporated in the training module could have been delivered with all the facilities now available within the institute. They perceived the time management in a better way and programme management with the internal arrangements. While, the Dean insisted on conducting the training programme outside the college environment.

The objectives of this training programme was to imbibe group culture, eliminate inhibition, develop mutual understanding, encourage team attitude, inculcate self awareness, induce leadership qualities, conscious-responsible behaviour, create work motivation and goal orientation. More than an ice breaking session, the programme visualizes and envisaged the development of individual mission statement from each student, that help them to orient themselves to achieve personal goals integrating professional goal.

The journey started at 8.35am in the morning. The bus was supposed to reach at 10.30am at Kuttikkanam Hilly Valley Resort. The students had to board from different places and because of some contingency situation in between the journey the bus had to halt at various places and got delayed by one hour. The bus reached only at 11.30 at to Kuttikkanam. The commencement of the training programme was delayed by one hour. Against the preplanned schedule the students were asked to engage in the training and development programme after having a cup of mango juice. The students were asked to attend the training programme leaving their luggage and belongings inside the bus. As per the direction of the Dean student started attending the training programme. The two trainers who were been waiting for the commencement of their programme could only start their programme after the late arrival of the students.

The first session started with grouping exercise, name-calling exercises, clapping exercises, voice based exercises and outbound song development exercises. The students got a large amount of opportunity for mutual understanding and developing many insights like importance of team work, attention, listening, awareness, concentration, leadership by removing inhibition in day to day interaction with their peers. The training programme was supposed to finish at one O'clock in the after noon for lunch. But the training programme went on till 2.15pm with the singing exercises. The lunch started at 2.25pm and ended at 3.O' clock. The afternoon session started only at 3.15pm. The delayed programme thus went on deviating from its preplanned schedule. The students had to take lunch, fulfill their basic needs, and settle down their luggage in their respective rooms in a short time.

The second phase of training programme went on till 7.15pm on the same day. The trainer engaged students in several group activities. The activities in the training programme had induced better learning exposure and insight on innovation and creativity in students. The trainers had to run their activities beyond the stipulated time frame. Mean while the CEO of the institute and an Academic Council member visited the training programme. The Academic Council member was from USA. After the training session without having any short break the Professor from abroad conducted another 45 minutes session. The students were not informed about the new session. Soon after the session, the CEO also joined the programme. The entire programme thus went on till 8 O' clock. Considering the hectic Schedule, the Dean informed the students that there wouldn't be any campfire activity based on the scheduled programme. Infact, the students were awaiting for the campfire for better interaction and relaxation. But, after the dinner, the decision on campfire changed again and the Dean informed the students that there would be campfire. The students were surprised to see the change in activities in every moment. The campfire that was conducted couldn't serve the purpose since there was heavy wind. The students could go to sleep only after 11 O' Clock.

The Dean informed one of the faculty members that he has cancelled his programme on the second day and that she would have to run the programme. As per the instruction she started better preparation to run the training for more hours. She had to spend more time during night to organize one and a half-hour training module on communication skill. Due to the modifications in the programme schedule at every moment the students started asking about the surety of the module to the teachers. Since the Dean had charted the programme they showed their inability to express anything. They reserved their comment.

The second day programme started with the Yoga and meditation programme at 7.15. The proposed time was 7.00am. More over there was no sufficient space for the 50 students to undergo yoga and meditation. Hardly 27 students underwent the yoga and meditation and the rest of them had to wait in the restaurant sitting idle. Since the Dean himself held yoga and meditation programme he couldn't engage students in any of the activities. More over the faculty members were not instructed to do anything. The Dean taught few steps of Pranayaama and training of meditation within a period of 45 minutes.

The second module started soon after the breakfast at 9.30am, though it was supposed to start at 9.00am. The lady faculty started her training module on communication with the assistance of other faculty members. She conducted training module with jumble words in group wise. The individual presentation of three groups on their jumbled words in right form and forming of a sentence by their on their own completed at 11.00am. Hardly 15 minutes to complete the programme with the remaining two groups' individual presentations and leader presentations. The lady faculty was asked to wind up the module immediately leaving it incomplete. She was disappointed by the interference of the Dean after being told that she would be in charge of the entire program for the day. The Dean started a movie 'IQBAL' soon after the 'incomplete communication' module. The hall faced a problem with the sound system. The service trainees of the resort tried to get the sound system run. But they failed in their effort. The films started only at 11.30am without proper sound effect. The students didn't get enough time for break and relaxation. The tea/coffee and the snacks were supplied right in their seat and the programme run with shortage of time. The film ended halfway without serving the purpose, since the programme had to be finished at 1 O'Clock in the afternoon.

The students were given assignment on presenting what they have learned from the film and the Dean asked them present it on next day. At 1 O' Clock he started another training programme on rabbit and tortoise. The students received yet another assignment to right the game. More over he asked all of them to submit their learning from the entire programme.

The programme ended at 3.00pm beyond the stipulated time. In the second day all the activities went on half way. Half of the students didn't get the benefit of yoga and meditation. The communication programme had to be stopped half way. The film was played without sound effect and stopped on half way. The Rabbit and Tortoise also had to wind up half way. The students openly shared their displeasure and discomforted with the programme. They complained the faculties for not giving proper attention on their basic needs.

The entire training programme went on with mixed impression from the students and the faculty members. Some of the faculties lodged complaint against the Dean to the Director about their concerns and anxieties on Dean's behaviour. They reported to the Director that they were mere the spectators of the entire programme. They complained that many of the faculty members who have good training experience in prestigious business schools and corporate sectors were ignored. They felt that the programme was imposed on them rather than incorporating their suggestions and ideas. There were poor communication between faculty members and the management.. Only a few faculty members, who were close to the Dean, received the information about the programme and others were not informed. Others came to know the programme only a day before the event. Everything went on with the centralized ideas of the Dean. He behaved just like a dictator. The faculty members requested the Director for his immediate intervention in the matter and take adequate action. The Director called the Dean immediately and asked him to send an immediate report incorporating faculty members and student's opinion in this mater.

The Dean was annoyed when he came to know that faculty members reported the matter to the Director. Director further entrusted one of the faculty members to give a detailed report incorporating the integrated views of faculty members, trainers and students on this programme within 24 hours. More over he ordered an enquiry at administrative level to know the cost incurred in the entire programme.

Questions

1. Failure to plan is planning to fail,' how do you comment on this statement with reference to the case study?
2. How do you relate absence of planning in the present day business context?
3. Discuss the importance of planning in a successful event in the organisation?
4. Discuss the significance of participation in formulating the plans. How do you ensure participation of people in the planning exercise?
5. To what extend decision-making is important in organizing any event or programme?
6. How do you realize the importance of Organizing and Coordination?
7. Delegation and decentralization is the Key to organisation effectiveness. Elucidate.
8. What is the decision making style of the Dean?
9. Must Leaders actively and intentionally motivate their subordinates? With reference to Dean's Directive approach elucidate.
10. 'Motivation is the Key to management.' How the Dean's decision making style affect the motivation and participation of the faculties in this case?
11. Discuss the importance of Information sharing, which is key to effective management of training programmes?
12. Discuss the leadership traits of Dean in this case study.
13. Assertiveness is the key quality required for managers. How far the lady teacher is assertive in her life?
14. In the initial stage of organizational Development do you feel that participation from the faculties are not essential?
15. If you will be in the Deans position how you plan and manage this training programme?
16. Keep in mind management principles, management functions, management approaches, principles of communication, work motivation and leadership theories, develop a plan of action for the effectiveness of training and development programme.

17. Compare the style of management in military organizations and educational institution. Differentiate the managerial approaches and leadership style in these two settings.

CASE 2

SPAN OF MANAGEMENT

Baron Zink Ltd a large-scale private sector industrial establishment has been running with profit for the last one decade. The company had a good marketing network and sales force all over the country. The organisation had divided the entire marketing region into six divisions like East, West, North, South, Central and North East. Kiran Kumar aged (38) is in charge of marketing, Southern region. As a marketing manager he is very competent, hardworking and committed to his work and the organisation. The culture of the organisation widely held employees and employers competency, skill and knowledge of employees to get better reward in the organisation. The company management has better impression upon the performance of Kiran. Kiran has to maintain a manageable sales force of Southern region. Though the Southern territory was little wide for networking, with the help of his sales force he maintained the entire region competing with other companies.

Kiran maintained a mentor-portage relationship with subordinates and engaged himself in solving many of the personal and professional problems with his sales force. He also made himself available to his sales and marketing team at any hour for quarries and concerns for strategic decision making. He usually conducts regional level meeting with his marketing and sales force to get better feedback about the product, quality, design, price, demand competition and fluctuating market environment etc. He tried to conduct market research to get information about the changes in the market. As the number of sales force members was manageable to him he made close contact with the group. By developing informal relationship and communication channels he believed that better superior-subordinates relationship could produce better results in the performance level. Kiran was excellent in developing better marketing strategies compared to other territory mangers since he was getting current information from his sales force about the market fluctuations and changes. The culture of the organisation promotes performance and competency. Kiran maintained a retention strategy of recognition and appreciation through monitory and non-monitory reward system. Under him almost 7 middle level managers and 21 junior level managers were working. He used to conduct weekly performance meeting with his subordinate level managers and strictly followed follow-up strategies. Based on the meeting he used to direct their subordinates about the marketing methods that are to be changed and new strategies to be adopted. During his close interaction with the sales force members he used to extend positive strokes to improve their performance. Since the sales force and the span of management were manageable to Kiran in the southern region he could manage his region with better sales and profit. The top level management didn't have any objection with his way of dealing with his sales force.

Mohan Kumar aged (42) Marketing Manger of central division has resigned from his post since he got better opportunity in one of the companies in North. The Central division was running with profit but not in par with other regions. Since the company was in a critical situation the management asked Mr. Kiran to take additional responsibilities of the central region.

The central division covers many areas more than Northern region. The task was challenging to him. Kiran was unaware of the marketing network, market conditions, market fluctuations, competition of local market products and the sales force. Since the company asked only for a stopgap arrangement, for one-month time for the selection of new manager, he said 'yes' to the management. He started managing two divisions. Thus two territories, two sales force and two set of subordinate managers came under his guidance and management. He found difficulty in conducting regular follow-up meetings with the middle level managers, junior level managers and the sales force of two territories. Many times he was delayed in getting to know the marketing problems of new territory and existing territory, because of that he failed to take strategic decisions in both territories. More over, he couldn't maintain the mentor portage relationship that he practiced with his sales force and the managers.

Mr. Mohan Kumar followed centralized decision-making process in his territory. The span of management was very limited. He had only ten mangers to manage huge territory. The number of sales staff was high when compared to South division. When the regular follow-ups and the meeting started he has faced difficulty to understand many of the marketing problem faced by the sales force in the central division. More over he couldn't develop good interaction and interrelation with his central division sales force because of hectic work schedule in a limited time span. The members of central sales force had the fear and anxiety about the new Marketing Manager (Kiran) who took charge of their territory. There were many organisational situations where Kiran could not control his functional interventions and organisational behaviour. He observed the superior level performance and the target accomplishments of his sales force, compared to the central division. He realized one thing that when he took up central division, he has lost control over his own sales forces of Southern region. He couldn't find enough time to maintain the relationship that he had once developed with his own sales force and the managerial members. The situation reached up to such a state that neither he could control his own regional sales force nor the new central sales force.

Periodical review of six regions happened in the month of July. The top level management recognizes the fact that the performance of the two territories viz., Central and South fell drastically within a period of three months. The wise president of marketing Division called Kiran and asked explanation for the poor performance. Kiran reported that he took up the additional responsibility of new division only for one month. He was expected to move back to his division after One month. He further informed the management that the arrangement made in the marketing division was only temporary. He took charge of the Central division as it gives sufficient time for management to recruit new manager in the vacant position. The company delayed the appointment. The two - territory was not manageable for Kiran to handle. More over the span of management was unaffordable to single manager. The report of Kiran was not satisfactory to management.

Within a period of one week the company appointed a marketing manager in the Central division. The top management took back the responsibilities of Central division from Kiran and handed over the same to the new Marketing manager. Kiran found himself highly satisfied with the management's decision that at least he can extend better functional performance on his own division.

Questions

1. Differentiate job enrichment, job enlargement and span of management?
2. Do you believe that management style influence the business operations? Differentiate the management style of Mohan Kumar?
3. How the span of management affects managerial control at operational level?
4. Will you agree with the statement that 'higher the span of management lower the flow of information and communication with subordinates'?
5. The company could have avoided the loss of surplus.' Elucidate.

CASE 3

AUTHORITY AND RESPONSIBILITY

Lilly-Lilly Pharmaceutical is a leading multinational pharmaceutical company located in Central Bangalore having a turn over of Rs 300 Crore. The company has largely 1500 employees and about 200 managers. The managerial level consists of senior, middle and junior level Managers. Out of 200 managers 10% are at senior level, 30% are at Middle level and the rest of them are junior level managers. The shop floor level consists of the workers at plant, production, instrumentation, electrical, lab, etc.

The company obtained the trust and confidence of the employees by following employee friendly policies and norms. The culture of the organisation followed employee supportive leadership, objective feedback, open communication, performance based reward system, and better authority and responsibility at functional level. The organisation consists of trade unions, but they support management with constructive contributions in business operations and management. They intervened only on problems with severe concerns. There was congenial relationship between employees and employers in this organisation. The morale of the workers was very high since there is cordial industrial relations, supportive leadership and effective management approaches. The employees observed high consideration and relationship orientation in the task performance.

The company also decided to go for expansion and extension program with the launch of new products. The management has decided to select few highly committed and hardworking workers from the shop floor level and promote them to manager's level and assign them these tasks on new product design and development. The management have of the impression that these employees have better understanding on the lacunas and pitfalls on the present products and these worker managers with the help of existing workforce can develop new products as an experimental effort. The management selected five young workers from the shop floor level and promoted them to the manager's level. The morale of the employees was increased by knowing the promotion news. The newly selected managers were sent for training and development programmes and prepared them to take up the task. These new managers were sent back to shop floor level with the newly assigned task of product design and development. The company has given them 6 months soon after training and development period in the allotted task.

These new managers were unaware of the authorities and power of managers since they came from the worker background. They were not aware of how to make effective use of power, authorities and responsibilities towards their fellow workers. They were workers before one month and they have sent back to their fellow workers with a new title of managers. The worker group consists of many old employees and with them they find difficult to use their authorities and responsibilities. Many of the hardworking and committed workers have discontent on the selection of these new managers by ignoring them. They have shown their non-cooperative attitude towards these new managers. The workers started calling them as 'worker manager.' These young managers found the situation pretty difficult to manage. Even in the difficult atmosphere they started their assignment with commitment. Many days they have spent more than working hours in the assigned task.

The management made a periodical review on the work progress of these new manages with their workers. The management came out with information about the project that the new managers could accomplish only 10% of the allotted task in a period of two months as against the expected out put of 40%. The information about the work group led them to go for an enquiry into the matter with an immediate concern. They came out with an informative report that the new managers were reluctant to use their power, authority and responsibility to plan and organize the work and coordinate and control their workers in the task accomplishment. The workers under these new managers were not ready to accept the new managers since they once were workers and then they turned into managers. Some of the new managers didn't have the analytical and research orientation that would help in the product design and development. The report forwarded to the senior level manages. They concluded the matter in the report that the newly elected, managers are good in routine works but not in higher responsibility tasks. The new managers didn't have that much analytical and research skills to develop a new product. The training and development have little impact on the new managers in their effective utilization of authority and responsibilities. More over the workers at the shop floor level had shown their non-cooperative attitude to the new managers because they found discrepancy in the selection and promotion of workers to the managerial level. Lack of adjustment with the new job responsibilities, role stress and role conflict are additional factors contributed to their failure in the assigned task.

The senior level managers show greater concern on the issue. They observed severe problems in the extension and expansion programme. They accepted the mistake of selection and promotion of new managers with preconceived assumptions and notions. They realized the important role of researchers, scientists, market analyst and many others who involvement in the product development. Since the matter affected the morale and involvement of the workers at the shop floor level they wanted an immediate intervention in the issue. Since stringent measures like de-promotion affects the morale and commitment of the workers they found it difficult to take some measures on these new managers. Without getting a proper solution in this matter the senior level managers refer the case to the HRD department.

Questions

1. How authority and responsibility is important in management of workers at shop floor level?
2. How you perceive the role of accountability in the effective use of authority and responsibility?
3. If you were an HR manager how you resolve the crisis without affecting the morale of employees?
4. If you were an HR manager how you resolve the crisis without the intervention of trade unions?
5. Will you agree with the statement that 'hard work and commitment' are not substitute to 'research and analytical skill'?
6. How you interpret justified use of authority in getting done through and with people?
7. To what extend the selection process accountable to you if you are an employee at shop floor level?

CASE 4

PERPETUAL DISTRIBUTIONSHIP

Wane Software is a global scientific & engineering solutions provider offering its customers with products, consulting, training and R&D. Wane Software has a cumulative global user base of over 360,000 in leading corporations (including several Fortune 500 companies), government agencies and academic institutions. It is significantly present in 39 countries worldwide through a network of direct offices and distributors/resellers.

Mr. Devaraj is a Business Development Manager in Crane Tech India Private Ltd, Pune. He is working in Crane Tech India Private Ltd, for the past 8 years. He is one of the efficient Business Development Executives who takes in charge of abroad business operations for the firm. The firm has arranged a business meeting in London. The meeting was so urgent that Mr. Devaraj has to attend the business meeting.

He has to take a flight to London from Mumbai at 11 pm on 10th October 2009 to a business meeting. Just as he left Pune by train at 3.15 pm, for Munbai on 10th October 2002 the Pune office receives a fax from London stating that "very important message for Mr. Devaraj to bring along the sample and papers dispatched by parcel by Air India." The firm office in London made it very clear that the document which Mr. Devaraj need to be collected and brought into as it is very important for our discussion'. Mr. Devaraj was going to London, for the finalization of a 'Sole distributorship in India' of a London manufactured product.

Mr. Kiran plunged into action just leaving a message to his boss, he picked up the fax message, went to the courier service and picked up the airway bill which was then just arrived. He took a taxi and proceeded to Mumbai. He reached Air India Freight office at about 9.pm. The staff working there refused to deliver the parcel as the office time was over at 5.30pm and the delivery register has been closed for the day. Now it is 9.30pm Mr. Devaraj unaware of the message or the happening is already at the air port. In another 45 minutes he will be inside pleading with the Air India flight staff but of no avail. But it is important that the material should reach Mr. Devaraj at the airport as this negotiation will finally result into a perpetual distribution ship contract or it will fall through.

Questions

1. Discuss in detail and advice Mr. Kiran about the perpetual distribution ship contract.

CASE 5

COPYRIGHT ISSUE

Mr. Thomas George invents a 'music software,' and calls it "Rampster". He gives this software to his friends. If it is once loaded in a computer, a person could request for a song. What the Rampster software does is an online search of other computers, which not only have the Rampster software, but also the song, requested for. Once such a computer is identified, the two computers could then "transfer" the requested music files in MP3 format. Mr. Felix Abraham is the CEO of Microsound a music company. On behalf of Microsound, Mr. Felix Abraham files a "suit for permanent injunction", praying for a total ban on the Rampster software as he claims that the software is facilitating the infringement of copyright in music, the copyright over which belongs to companies such as Microsound.

Questions

1. As a business lawyer engaged in management operations how would you decide the case?
2. What would be your decision to ban the software?
3. If you ban or not ban what would be your supporting reasons that substantiate your stand?
4. Discuss the case thoroughly in relation to labour laws and its terminologies. Find out effective solution.

CASE 6

BUSINESS PLAN

Maxwell Times Ltd., a Swiss collaboration company has opened a new plant 50 kms away from Pune with an initial investment of 60 crores to make watch cases. They cater mainly to Titan, HMT and other wrist watch makers in India and are therefore, extremely vigilant about quality, aesthetics and changing designs. The new project which they have started is in the still developing MIDC area with no municipal transport facilities (PMT) and state transport facilities (MSRTC) for conveyance to and fro Pune. There are water and accommodation problems and the tahsil level township nearest to the plant is 18 kms further from the site towards Ahmednagar. Most of the plant and machinery are imported.

The company started commercial production in 1991. They did extensive manpower planning and work study to prepare their human resource requirements. Accordingly, the company, now in November 1992 requires 200 fresh candidates in the age group of 18–22 years for various trades as mentioned below who should be operative by February 1993.

	Category	*Nos.*
1.	Turners (ITI / NCTVT passed)	20
2.	Millers (ITI / NCTVT passed)	6
3.	Fitters (ITI / NCTVT passed)	58
4.	Grinders (ITI / NCTVT passed)	4
5.	SSC passed (Physics & Maths) boys	97
6.	SSC passed (Physics & Maths) girls	15
	Total	200

The company is very conscious about quality control and they therefore need qualified technicians with aptitude to operation precision jobs. They are offering a year's training with a stipend of Rs.1000/- followed by Rs.2000/- and benefits in the second year.

They have a period of two months within which they have to complete the entire process of recruitment and selection– which consists of 2 psychological tests i.e the Psycho Dynamic Test (PDT) and the Neuro Muscular Test (NMT) interview and medical examination.

The local Sarpanch demands that the local youths be recruited and earlier after having administered the psychological test twice to the local population, some candidates have been selected to the ratio of suitability of 1:38. The company also has a policy of recruiting people only from Maharashtra.

The company is weighing whether to do this project themselves or to sub-contract it to a consulting organization.

1. How will you advise the company?
2. If you decide to subcontract, what will be the terms and conditions?
3. On what criteria will you select the consulting agency?

All the above matters pending.

Questions

1. Develop a media selection and sourcing strategy and an advertisement to be released in the newspapers which should cover all Maharashtra state.
2. Determine the costs involved in this phase.
3. The past experiences show that the rejection rate after PDT is 80% after the NMT is 50% interview rejection rate is 40% medical rejection rate is 35% the joining rate is 80% and the retention rate is 40%.c
4. Prepare an induction manual for the selection personnel.

Case 7

PROBLEMS OF MIGRATED PLANTATION WORKERS

I am Sali, a 30-year-old plantation woman worker, staying at one of the private management owned, Thellar Tea Estate*, in Munnar. My Native is at Idukki, one of the high range district of Kerala states. My husband is Verghese, a regularized plantation worker in the Thellar Tea Estate. We have two daughters, the elder one studying in 5th standard and the younger one, a one-year baby. My family members are six in number along with my parents and are staying in the permanent quarter of the Thellar estate.

Long back, my father Verghese came here, in search of job. During those days the Thellar Tea Estate was facing acute shortage of workers for plantation labour. Though, the management recruited many workers from Teni, Thirunelveli, Thengashi like places in the Tamil Nadu state, still, the plantation labour required more workers. Since the tea plantations in Munnar were facing acute shortage of workers, my father easily got plantation work in Thellar Tea Estate. More over the plantation management were ready to provide the basic facilities like food, shelter, clothing and a reasonable wage to the workers to ensure their continuous stay in the tea plantations. Frankly speaking, we don't have too much property in our native place, at Idukki in Kerala. My father sold all the assets he had at Kerala and migrated to Thellar Tea Estate as and when he got a job and small quarter for permanent settlement. The only difficulty we were to face during those days was the chilling climate of the tea plantations.

I would like to appreciate my work and tell you that work was joy to plantation workers in those days, when they were migrated here. Waking up in the morning, walking long distance in the chilled climate with other workers, by sharing each other's pleasure and pains, going to field and engage in their work collectively. We were enjoyed the climate and the work environment, since it gives a peace of mind and happiness in the work. A better living condition, a better wage and a better work environment thus were given us a pleasurable emotional state. We were accustomed to the chilling climate and enjoyed the nature of work.

Let me give a brief view about our work. Morning 8 O' clock we have to reach at filed. To reach there in time we all have to wake up at 5 O' clock in the morning. It is my responsibility to prepare the food for the six members in the family. Since my mother in law is suffering from acute asthma I have to specifically take care of her food and health too. My husband has to reach at field at around 7.30 in the morning. Since the field is 4-5 kilometers away from the quarters I have to leave at 7.00 in the morning. My nature of work is to collect the tender leaves of the tea plant ('Kilunth Nullal') from the field. I have to collect 18 kilos of tender leave every day from the field. For additional collection of leaves incentives are given. For additional collection of tender leaves, which is beyond 18 Kg, the management fixes 50ps/Kg as incentives. Since money is a motivational factor for daily sustenance, we used to collect 25-30 kgs of leaves every day. My husband and I are getting better income from the plantation work.

As I have already mentioned, in the past, management was so keen in making provision of all the welfare, health facilities and financial assistance to the labourers. The management believes that the healthy worker is very important for plantation work. The management has given raincoats and woolen clothes to the workers during rainy season. They have given assistance to employees by making provision of 50 Rs for collection of food grains from the ration shop. Though, some time we had to face delay in the payment but management made the part payment to take care of the family needs. The management was prompt in giving incentives to the additional work. There is no unnecessary hassle between workers and management there is a trust on the part of labourers towards the management. The union practices are constructive and supportive to the management. The management is so considerate to the workers as they are committed to work and shown their integrity to the organisation. They have given assistance to the education of the children. Company started a crèche near by the quarters and appointed some supervisory ladies to look after the children of workers. The management is giving free food and milk to the children in the crèche. They provide company vehicle to take the sick workers to the hospitals, in the emergency. For the permanent worker they initiated the provident fund also. The workers have high trust and confidence on the management. People can share their pain and pleasure to the management since there is congenial relationship exists between workers and management.

Let me tell you, the entire crisis started as soon as the change of leadership has happened five years back. The past leaders and management have gone. The new management and leadership have taken up the estate. The plight of the laborers started as and when the change of ownership happened. The new management communicated to the workers that the organisation is facing the severe financial crisis of rupees 5 corers because of the too much of welfare provisions and benefits have given to the workers, by the past management. They informed the workers their difficulty to increase their payment, in the coming 7 years to curb the financial out lay. To curb the financial liability it is intimated by the management to the workers that the organisation will have to go for downsizing. They announced the decision to go for voluntary retirement scheme to the permanent employees. To the temporary workers, they asked to leave the company within a period of 5 months. They also have taken decision to cut down current welfare facilities in the coming years. Management asked the workers to collect more kilos of tea leaves every day and they increased the working hours. They asked the workers to work more to secure their job in future. The change of leadership has thus inculcated 'change of belief' among workers and they feel insecure about their work and future.

Management rescheduled the working time from morning 7 O' clock to 3 O' Clock. Labourers have to leave their home to work at 6.30 in the morning. The workers have to reach in time in the field. They reduced the wages of the latecomers. Management tightened the work supervision. The informal sharing and social interaction are not entertained in the field. The supervisors started using abusive languages on workers in their task performance. The rebel labourers are sent to distance places, in order to give punishment massage to the other workers. The family members who work together are separated in the work, to avoid unnecessary interaction at work. They increased the minimum collection of tea leave from 18 kg to 25 Kg. The casual leave, sickness leaves etc, like available leaves have banned. No consideration is given to the members who are ill. More over, giving raincoats and woolen in the rainy season, to the workers is scraped.

The Management has taken several additional steps to curb the excess financial outlay. These can be detailed as follows.

- Weekly 50 Rs for the ration allowance is stopped.
- Reduced the present wage from 80 rupees per day to 53 rupees per day.
- Incentive system is stopped
- Delayed payment to the workers
- Delayed bonus
- Running crèche for the workers children is stopped
- Voluntary retirement scheme is announced
- Union activities is totally denied
- Educational assistance to the worker's children stopped
- Women education not entertained

- Those families among which three members are employed in the plantation are asked to reduce it to two members.
- Company vehicles are not allowed to take the sick labourers to the hospital
- Work is prominent than welfare

I would like to tell you some strange incidents happened against the workers, widely supported by the present management.

- The management sought the help of goondas" to evacuate the plantation workers from the quarters.
- Union leaders are silent to the management actions
- Women labourers faced sexual harassment at work
- New recruitment even after downsizing
- Indiscrimination on the wages between male and female workers
- Stringent disciplinary measures
- Power supply is cut down to the laborer's quarters.

Let me share, how the change of leadership has created fear and anxiety among workers in the plantation. The change of leadership and the attitude of management developed deep insecurity among workers. The delayed payment of their wages, severely affected to materialize worker's existential needs. Many a time workers have to borrow money from moneylenders to meet their basic needs. The education of the workers children is now at stake. The sickness status of the estate labourers is going up. Since the work pressure is heavy and there is no return, many workers are decided to quit their job. Specifically, those who migrated from distant places are the victims of these stringent measures taken by the management. Neither they have any house in their native nor here in the estate. Their job is insecure and future of their family is at stake. The union leaders show their indirect support to the management in many steps they have taken. There is high dilution of the trust and confidence; the workers have on the union leadership. The worker's feel insecure, as there is no social and economic support to meet their existential needs either from the management or from the union organisation.

The workers believe that all the steps management has taken to implement their own whims and fancies. They wanted to appoint their own labourers. All the work pressure thus created is to evacuate the present labourers from the plantation and there by appoint new labourers. They still believe that the company is running with profit.

I would like to tell you our concern. Look upon the workers of the tea plantations. We oozed our sweat and blood to the organisation to which we work for. In return company is creating severe hardships to our day-to-day life. We don't have any one in our native places. Where will we go if management knocks us out from here? How will our children study? Who will look after our sick parents and relatives? How should we protect them? How we care our children? We don't know what to do...No job, no wage and there by no life to the plantation labourers.

You might have heard the strikes in the plantation that went on smoothly in the last month. Let me tell you that, the strike in the plantation is situational than intentional. In order to prevent management action against the workers, the plantation labourers of the Thellar Tea Estate united together one day and some of the workers emerged as leaders from within. They called one-day strike against the management pointing out the issues at work. But the management continued their reluctance further. The workers started one week strike. The workers are of the belief that, nothing to loose with this strike than some gains. In a 'do or die' situation there is no choice left to workers, but to fight against the management. The difference in the nature of strike here is that strike is done not for the luxurious needs but for getting the existential needs. We got the result we expected. When management realized the fact that the production is getting affected because of strike, they loosened their stand against the labourers, though with severe antagonistic attitude. The groups thus formed prevented further recruitment in the company. It blocked the company's move against the downsizing. Through negotiation, they ensured the fair wages to the plantation workers. They made an agreement with the management in the incentive system, and several other basic needs. Though management doesn't roll back majority of their stringent measures, they have shown their changes in their treatment and understanding.

Let me ask you few questions.... Why did the management compel workers to go for agitation to get the things done? Is 'strike' the only weapon to get justice here in this country for the workers? How do people look upon labour laws? Do the workers get any better living condition with the labour laws existing in the plantations? Who cares the plantation workers? Is the management here to fight with workers? Is this the real function of management? Is there any hope to the plantation labourers from the government side?

Leaving her several question aside....Sali ends up her 'story of agitation' here....

Questions

1. Discuss the plight of plantation labourers?
2. How the leadership style varied in this case. Relate the case with content theories and process theories of leadership.
3. What are the factors affecting the work motivation of plantation labourers?
4. How the work motivation and work behaviour is affected by the managerial approaches.
5. The membership of trade union organizations are reducing day by day' (HMS, BMS). Discuss the leadership issues.
6. Which are the areas in which management violates the Plantation Labour Act 1956?
7. Which are the areas in which management violates the Minimum Wages Act 1948?
8. Do you believe that leaders are born than made? Substantiate your comment?
9. Find out the reasons of collective workers movement?
10. Where there is no promotion and no work enrichment, how the workers motivation can be improved.

Case 8

RECRUITMENT AND SELECTION

Mr. Sreenivas (55) working as manager in Alfa Chemicals, a large scale industrial establishment engaged in the production of Phosphate and Sulphur. He has 30 years of experience in Alfa Chemicals. He has an excellent track record as Manager in Human Resources within the organization. Many times he got 'best employer award' to his excellent performance. His area of expertise is in recruitment and selection process, and the performance appraisal has been widely acknowledged.

The Information Technology division of Alfa Chemicals industry once faced acute shortage of manpower. Mr. Raj, Manager IT division put forward an immediate requirement of 10 employees in the IT division, to HR department, starting from junior level to senior level. When Mr. Sreenivas got the letter from Mr. Raj, in his department, he started processing it. To get it done, he approached many sources. He had gone through the data bank of company and considered 100 resumes for recruitment. He also informed the employees and employers of the organization, for the immediate requirement of 10 employees to facilitate the internal recruitment procedures. From the employees and employers of Alfa Chemicals he got around 150 applications with resumes. In addition to that in order to give an opportunity to candidates' external to the organization he gave an advertisement in several daily news papers viz., Times of India, Sakal, and Indian Express. From external sources he got around 350 applications. Almost 600 candidates, including internal and external applicants, applied for 10 vacant post. To ensure the reliability and dependability of the process, Sreenivas made his personal scrutiny at all levels, in the recruitment and selection process. Since the entire department function as a team in HR, all the members trust each other and extended their valuable contribution in the recruitment and selection.

The department conducted a preliminary interview in order to made first screening process and filter the number of applicants. After the first screening process the HR department reduced the number of applicant list from 600 to 500 applicants. He conducted a written test and group discussion and there by reducing the number of applicants to 300. These 300 candidates then exposed to one hour psychometric test and out of which 50 candidates selected for the final interview. From the final interview, 10 candidates finally selected. The entire process of recruitment and selection took almost 3 months. The selected candidates list were then forwarded to the top management for the final approval. HR department informed the candidates that the appointment letters will be sent to those who are selected for the post.

Sreenivas approached several time to the top management to get final approval of list of candidates for the IT department. Sreenivas informed the IT department also that there is a delay in the announcement of the final list as the top management would like to take some more time. He waited almost 4 weeks. But, no reply at all. Mr. Raj, the IT manager every day enquired about the latest information of the final list of the candidates and tentative date of induction. Sreenivas faced the difficulty to make any comment on the subject as there was no information from the top management. HR department had to answer many phone calls from out side and inside the organization, as recruitment involved candidates from inside and outside. The employers and employees of the industry, whose relatives got into the final selection process, became regular visitors of the HR department, asking for the finalist. Sreenivas called a meeting of HR team members and once again made a close verification of the entire process. But he couldn't find any fault in any of the recruitment and selection process. As the time went on he became more suspicious about the delay in the announcement of the result.

When the problem became so crucial Sreenivas got direction from the top management to meet Mr. Kartik, General Manager, one of the top officials in the organization. Mr.Kartik asked the entire process of recruitment and selection that made on IT professionals. Sreenivas furnished the entire details of the process in a precise report. Mr. Kartik read the entire report and soon after made a direct comment that the recruitment and selection process that for IT professionals need to be cancelled as he observed some discrepancies in the process made by his department. He further directed Sreenivas that the vacancies have to be filled through contract basis and no permanent vacancies to be made in these positions, for one year. Further he informed Sreenivas that another recruitment process was to be done from external candidates and no internal application to be entertained. Sreenivas couldn't agree with the Mr. Kiran comment on his department's inefficiency in the recruitment and selection process. For a while he thought about quitting the organization, as he faced a baseless allegation from the top management. Till date there is no black mark in his functional dissemination. On many occasion he helped the industry to find out the best possible solutions in order to tackle the many manpower crisis. Sreenivas became so depressed and felt quiet unhappy about the decision taken by the management.

Mr. Sreenivas called an urgent meeting of his subordinates and communicated the management decision and directives. He shared with the team members that the management had greater dissatisfaction on the recruitment and selection process done by the department. He enquired whether there was any mistake done by them, in the process. All members denied the probability of any mistake. As there were clear norms and regulations related to each step and there was no dual command, they found no possibility of creeping errors in the selection process. In the meeting he informed his subordinates that the management freezes the appointment process for IT professionals and asked for external recruitment on contract basis. It was shocking news to the members. They asked several questions to get a proper clarification from Sreenivas. As Mr. Sreenivas himself was unaware of the reasons behind the decision of management about his inability to give a proper reply in this regard. Sreenivas also informed this matter to Mr. Raj.

During the evening hours, in the same day, Sreenivas got a call from Mr. George, one of his senior-level Managers, with whom he had friendly and informal relationship. Mr. George asked Srinivas to come to his cabin. As per the call Mr. Sreenivas met George in his cabin. George enquired on his family and many unofficial matters in the informal interaction. Half an hour later, Mr. George enquired on the recruitment and selection process of IT professionals. He shared with George all those things happened with top management. Leaving aside the informal interaction, George initiated formal discussion with Sreenivas. He told Sreenivas that the selected list of IT professionals consisted two names, Mr. Avdesh and Mr. Praveen, they are the relatives of two trade union leaders of the organization. The management felt that being the relatives of two trade union leaders, in the long run, they could be a threat to organization. It may create an image that the trade unions still have a control over the decision making process in organization. Further, the hold of trade union may expand if this selection process materializes. Mr. Geroge informed Sreenivas that management didn't have any doubt on the dependability and exactness of the recruitment processes that done by the department of HR.

George further informed Sreenivas that as per the intimation from top management he called Mr. Sreenivas and briefed the undercurrents of this episode. The entire news was shocking to Mr. Sreenivas. He didn't know that the management decision had this much of undercurrents. After hearing entire story Sreenivas become so silent and returned to his cabin.

While sitting inside his cabin, he made a silent comment that, "what a useless effort.

Questions

1. What are the undercurrents of selection process in Alfa Chemicals?
2. How management decision justifies management effort in the maintenance of harmonious industrial relation?
3. Do you believe that as HR Manager, Mr. Sreenivas failed to gather direct and indirect information about the candidates?
4. How 'cancellation of appointment' decision that affect the moral of organizational members?
5. How you interpret the dilemma of HR managers have to face in such kind of situations.
6. What would be your decision if you have to face such situation?
7. Do you believe that trade unions have 'quota' in appointments?
8. How the decision affect the reduction of wastages and improvement of resources.
9. Is the decision reflecting management fear towards trade union or inability to develop a congenial industrial relationship within the organization?
10. How you interpret the silence of Mr. Sreenivas?

Case 9

SELECTION PROCESS OR TERMINATION

Green Finishing School (GFS) was formed with an objective to increase the number of employable Graduates and Post graduates for the Indian industry. With millions of graduates and post graduates available for recruitment, the Indian industry is facing with the problem of recruiting the employees ones which are surprisingly very few. The gap is yawning.

The gap between the number of Graduate and Post-Graduate students every year in the market vs. the number those can be employed by the Industry. With years of expertise in behavioral skill development and developing analytical and logical thinking, Green Finishing School (GFS) is one of the premier assessment and training companies in India. The services range from assessment services to consulting the training for the Corporate as well as Institutional sector.

The organisation has around 100 employees who are on regular employment. Based on their assignments they are well paid by the organisation. The company had a turn over of 50 Crores per annum. The employees have to work from 9.am to 6.pm. Since the Director of the organisation has to go for business trips for business canvassing he has decided to appoint one Deputy Director to supervise the business operations on day to day basis.

The Director had interviewed around 16 senior professionals for the position of Deputy Directors Position.

Finally he has short listed 3 candidates based on their expertise to handle the business operations. What made Mr. Gupta's profile different from that of other two was his experience in training and development, especially in area of soft skills, in addition to the business operations. Mr. Gupta requested for flexi timing for the post. But the Director had given him a choice of 11am to 6.pm. At the time of giving appointment letter the Director made it very clear the importance of Gupta's presence in handling business operations in office in his absence. Mr. Gupta also agreed the same with utmost integrity and keenness.

Mr. Gupta joined Green Finishing School (GFS) on 1st June 2002. For the first three years he had shown his punctuality, integrity, expertise in business operations and administration. He developed circle of friends in administration during these days, even the administrative staff members can handle his work in his absence. He got enough opportunity to train the students and corporate members during his regular work He enjoyed training more than business operation and administration. He earned more money from private trainings in corporate as well as in the institutions.

During his two year tenure in Green Finishing School (GFS) Mr. Gupta developed better circle of business relationship with many business schools and firms. He got plenty of expertise in handling pre-placement training programmes and consultancies to corporate. He started private training programmes and consultancies without knowing the parent company through the business contact that he developed. The Director of the company had greater faith on Mr. Gupta and he never suspects his integrity to the organisation. Mr. Gupta handled both assignments with his circle of friends and had given certain share to satisfy them.

One day the Director made a surprise visit to the company to over see the progress of a new assignment which they have got from a prestigious business school. He came to know that the Deputy Director is not in the organisation to handle this operation and deliver his responsibilities. He got to know from his close friends that Mr. Gupta started his own private training programmes and consultancies to various organisations through the contact he developed through the parent organisation. He came to know from the employees that Mr. Gupta is regularly irregular in the organisation. Without delaying his decision the Director decided to terminates him from the organisation with an immediate effect.

Next day morning, Mr. Gupta reported in the office. The Director asked him to resign from the position and the organisation. The Director briefed him about his irregularities and misconducts one by one and detailed his casual approach to handle the business operations. Mr. Gupta asked the Director further that he should have intimated these irregularities earlier. The Director said that he ought to know his higher level responsibilities, since he was a highly qualified person and holding a senior position in the organisation.

Mr. Gupta was not in a mood to accept the allegations against him. He replied to the Director that all the allegations against him was forged and not based on truth. The director also was not in state of mind to accept his clarifications. He informed Mr. Gupta that "if he didn't RESIGN his service he shall be TERMINATED with immediate effect. The organisation won't give any experience certificate for the past service in this organisation.

Perplexed Gupta RESIGNED.

Questions

1. How you see this case whether it as selection problem or employee attitude problem?
2. How can you justify the selection of Mr. Gupta as Deputy Director?
3. Do you believe that Mr. Gupta is to be terminated from the organisation?
4. How far trust and integrity matter in organisational life.
5. Discuss the group dynamics in this case which go against and go with the organisation in its growth towards stability and prosperity. .
6. How far the Director shows his responsibility in business operation?

Case 10

STRATEGIC RESTRUCTURING AND APPRAISAL

ABC consultancy is one of the prestigious training and development consultancies in Bangalore. The consultancy started its operations in Bangalore in 1995. The current turnover of the consultancy is 5 corers and it has 10 branches at different locations in Kerala.

The ABC consultancy consists of Board of Directors, Chairman, Vice Chairman, 7 directors and a staff representative. The Chief Executive is designated as Manager, under him there is an Asst. Manager Mr. Thomas who is BCom and has completed CA Inter. He is 49 years old. He joined the training and development consultancy on a salary of Rs.15,500/- and has gone upto Rs.35, 000/- in 2005. He looks after all the training and development concerns of their clients and allocates the resources for different events. Almost 12 staff members work under him.

Parallel to the Asst. Manager is the Office Manager Mr. Rajeev who is 53 years old. He looks after all the financial outlay and inlay of company. He joined the the training and development consultancy as a clerk on a salary of 8000/- Rs in 1995 which now stands at Rs.22, 000/-. The bank has 20 senior officers, 3 junior officers, 6 clerks drawing junior officers pay and 26 clerks in addition to the above managers. Selection of personnel has been on the basis of personal knowledge, family affiliation, political pressure, leniency etc and minimum qualification is being Degree. The company provides training and development programme to the interns and the internal employees at the entry level. Training is restricted to a 3 months course from a Bangalore based institute. Sponsorship is only at the discretion of Board of Directors. After 10 staff members, Board of Directors stopped sponsoring staff for this training programme. Those who underwent this training were given one extra increment.

Promotion is on the basis of seniority and in case one does not get the first promotion within 5 years, he is given a salary of junior officer without promoting him to that position. Performance appraisal is not being done nor is proper documentation available. The Chairman, Vice Chairman and another Director form the core group of the BOD that decided everything about the selection of employees.

Questions

1. How the case study reflects professionalism in managing people at work
2. How the performance appraisal system presently works and how it can be made effective.
3. How the selection process of the system works at present and how it can be professionalized.
4. Develop a plan of action that improve present condition of the consultancy that intern develop better development and profit to firm.
5. Critically evaluate the organisation structure of the company and suggest effective change if necessary. How employees can get be motivated through effective performance management system.

Case 11

PERFORMANCE APPRAISAL AND SELECTION PROCESS

The Ferrous Engineering Ltd., is a Pune based engineering company, their principal activities are to manufacture and sell internal combustion engines, diesel and gas generating sets and special purpose machines. The Group operates in two segments Engine Business and Others. Its products include sale and leasing of diesel power generating sets and allied equipment including operation and maintenance facilities of these equipments, hydraulic governors, engineering components, spare parts and accessories. The Group's plants are located at Maharashtra and Daman.

Mr Felix is the Director of Engineering Products in Electronic Equipment Company. The policy of the company is, it never entertains campus placements in the engineering colleges. Every year the company provides more than 100 projects to their engineering students. Based on the performance of the project trainees the company selects 50 students to their domestic and international engineering product development assignments.

The company HR conducts stringent selection process for the recruitment and selection of project trainees who require both managerial skills and engineering skills. The resume of the students are keenly reviewed by the selected engineers and the panel members from the top management since it inquire financial outlay and expectation of best performers. The HR department usually gives the engineering profiles to the panel member and they initially develop short listed students for the recruitment and selection process. The selection process consists of technical aptitude test, psychometric test, management aptitude test, group discussion and personal interview. The final approval of the selected list will be made by Mr. Felix personally himself through direct interviews to cross check all the comments and recommendations.

During the 6 month training cum project programme the engineering students receives class room study, and are taken around to each engineering functional areas to understand the parts, design, texture, materials, manufacturing, product development etc. The feed back from the supervisors are collected from each department about the training and progress of learning. The final decision to engage them in real time work is decided by Mr. Felix based on the performance appraisal and the personal interview conducted by him at the end of the project period.

What really bothered Mr. Sharma was that so many of the trainees who scored highest in technical and management aptitude tests, psychological test and personal interview didn't receive the highest evaluation from the functional supervisors, who worked with them in the past 6 months of their projects and training programmes for final placements. It was also clear that those trainees possessing the highest academic averages in the college, through out the semesters and the pre-university exams, didn't necessarily perform the best during their 6 month training programmes. The students lack both aptitude and attitude to perform their task effectively. The company thus didn't get number of right candidates for its final placement and further to that company lost the money they have invested to train and identify the future employees.

Based on the result of the training and project programmes of the last year, Mr. Felix was confused whether he should go with stringent selection process or hand pick those students who really does home work based on certain number of company assignment given on varied functional areas, by the company for the project and training programme. He was further got confused in providing training programmes to engineering students in their project period which inquire more financial out lay without providing adequate results. He called a meeting with his HR managers and team members to discuss this issue to understand the opinion of his members for a collective decision on project recruitment and selection process.

Questions

1. Critically evaluate the effectiveness of the project selection process engineers in Ferrous Engineering Ltd., Pune.
2. Where does the problem lies whether in the performance of the project trainees or in the recruitment of selection process.
3. Can you identify any problems with the decision making style of Mr. Sharma in this case content.
4. How do you relate the input and out put ratio for effective decision making process in procurement and development function?
5. Identify prospective intervention of training need assessment and training design for effectiveness and efficiency.
6. Critically analyze the reliability of supervisors report on the new entrants.

Case 12

INTERVIEW AND SELECTION

Prof. Ramarajan is working as Professor in HR in the Institute for Research, Management and Administration (IRMA), one of the prestigious institutes in Pune. He had a track record of 12 international publications, 24 national publications, one book, 10 research projects, vast experience in corporate training and teaching. His area of expertise is widely acknowledged in the teaching and training areas of Human Resource Development. Since his family settled at Hyderabad, he would like to switch over to one of the best institute in Hyderabad.

Quiet fortunately, he saw an advertisement in the times of India, in the month of May 2006, inviting vccancies for the faculty in the MSCI (Management Staff College, India), Hyderabad. Quiet enthusiastically, he applied for the post of faculty in HRD in MSCI. He came to know that MSCI had been all along engaged in imparting training for IAS, IFS, IRS, like professionals and the industrial managers. The institute is engaged in research and training, at large with the public sector industrial organizations and currently running programs in the areas of health management like MHA (Master of Hospital Management), PGDHA (Post Graduate Diploma in Hospital Administration and many certificate programs like, Urban Management, rural management, Water Management, Waste Management, Public Administration etc., for government staffs and the public sector managers etc.

In the month of May 10th 2006, Prof. Ramarajan had applied for the post of faculty in MSCI. After two months, in

July, he got a call letter from MSCI, indicating that he has been short listed for the post of SRF (Senior Research Fellow). Looking at the interview call letter he became quiet surprised and annoyed. MSCI has called him for SRF position, which is far below to his present position of Associate Professor. Since the interview call letter was sent by the Asst. Registrar MSCI, Prof. Ramarajan has tried to make a telephonic interaction with him. Prof. Ramarajan informed the Asst. Registrar that last 10 years he has been working as Assistant and Associate Professor of Human Resource Management in the Institute for Research Management and Administration (IRMA) in Pune and by getting a Salary of 35000/- with free accommodation and other allowances. The Asst. Registrar replied him immediately that they made a mistake in his case. He suggested him to send a concern letter to his office on the same day. He promised justice and fairness in this case by taking steps to forward this matter to the Director MSCI. As per his direction Prof. Ramarajan has forwarded a letter of concern to the Director MSCI.

On the other day he received an e-mail from the Asst. Registrar MSCI stating that he is invited for a presentation on 7th August and followed by that an interview with the MSCI board members, on 9th August, for the post of 'Faculty'. The e-mail communication asked him to report on 7th August 2006 in the MSCI, Bella Vista, Hyderabad. MSCI made entire arrangement for his accommodation in the Centre for Management premises at Banjara Hills. He gets a full furnished, air-conditioned-twin sharing room. The food and accommodation facilities were good enough to praise the organizers. Prof. Ramarajan came to know that for all of the candidates, accommodation arrangement has been made in the Centre for Management hostel itself. He gets into friendship with many candidates. There were candidates from IIMs, SP Jain, MDI, Symbiosis etc. He realized the severity of acute competition in the interview and in the presentation process. All of them were but anxious about the expectations of the institute, since there is no MBA program run by the institute, either for the corporate executives or for the students.

On 7th August, 2006, as per the directives, MSÇI has sent a vehicle to pick up three of the candidates, including Prof. Ramarajan from the Centre for Management hostel. The MSCI Bella vista campus has shown its majestic through its traditional buildings, infrastructure and elegance. When they reached, the Asst. Registrar welcome all of them. He directed to go to common hall and asked us to wait there. The first activity he did was distribution of travel and expenditure form to all of the candidates and asked to fill it and return to the administration for travel claim. As soon as we started filling the form, the IIM faculty got the first presentation call. He went on for the presentation. His presentation took almost 45 minutes. Every one sitting in the common hall was waiting him to gather information about the presentation. When he has come out of the board room, we observed his disappointed face. We enquired him about the presentation. He told others that the board conducted both presentation and interview together and the questions asked were not related to his academic expertise. The persoin from IIM has shared with others some of the questions that he recollected, which include,

1. Have you had any experience in corporate training and consultancy?
2. How much money you can pool from corporate training to the institute?
3. How much money can you pool from research project to the institute?
4. How much money can you pool can from corporate consultancy to the institute?

The IIM faculty added his personal comment in between that 'he don't know why the panel asked such kind of questions to a faculty who came from the prestigious institute of this country.' It is widely known factor that majority IIM faculties have been engaged in training and consultancies, in addition to teach their individual courses. He shared his apprehensions that MSCI do not have any plan to start MBA program here in Bella Vista and they required only people who can 'pump money' to institute.

The second candidate was called for the interview soon after the IIM fellow. He was one from IBS, Tamilnadu. His interview took about 40 minutes. He also mentioned that the 'presentation has little importance' in the interaction but they give more thrust to the 'interview,' which was not intimated in advance. The board asked him:

1. How much you are getting from ICFAI?
2. What are the functions you have to perform in ICFAI?
3. Do ICFAI conduct any training and development program?
4. Do they engage MDPs?
5. How much the institutes get from MDPs?
6. Which are the companies ICFAI consulted so far in Training and Development and Consultancy work?

He told us that there was no question from the power point presentation or from the academic expertise. They didn't ask any question from his international publications or from the teaching field. All others understood from his interaction that he became so disappointed with the interview experience.

With all this information, Prof. Ramarajan became frustrated. But he didn't lose his confidence. The Director gave warm welcome to Prof. Ramarajan. Before he started the presentation, the Director appreciated Prof. Ramarajan's qualifications and credentials and requested him to shorten the presentation, since they were running short of time. He told Prof. Ramarajan that the presentation is only for the analysis of communication skills. He further asked Prof. Ramarajan to finish it by 10 minutes. But Prof. Ramarajan felt bad about the request and resisted. He informed the board that if they could have intimated it in advance he could have reduced the number of PPT slides to the minimum. Though with disagreement, he followed the request of Director and started the presentation. But, within five minutes the interview board asked him to finish his presentation and sit for interaction. They started the question answer session.

1. How are you comfortable with training and development?

2. How many MDP program you have conducted in the last one year?
3. How much would you charge each individual participant in training?
4. To what extent would you share MDP amount with the institute?
5. What about research projects?
6. How many research projects you carried out in the past years?
7. How's the money-sharing proportion with the institute, on research projects?
8. If we appoint you as faculty, what would be yours revenue sharing mechanism to the institute?

Reaching no where, the interaction ended up with 'warm goodbye' from the Directors. Prof. Ramarajan became so annoyed about the presentation and the interview. The experience of him was not much different from that of other candidates. He came out with disappointment. All the other candidates circled him and enquired about his experience. He replied them that the experience of him was not much different from that of others. Both presentation and interview was finished.

By having a disturbed mind, the Prof. Ramarajan floated many questions in his mind;

- Why these people couldn't mention these requirements in the interview letter.
- 'If they would, we could have prepared better or avoid this travel.
- If they need trainers and consultants that indication should be mentioned in the advertisement or the interview call letter.
- The decision whether to attend or not to attend could also have been taken, without loosing these five man-days, if things would have been clear in the interview letter and the advertisement.

He concluded his interaction with others indicating that the institute objective of more on 'resource mobilization,' specifically 'fund mobilization,' than teaching.

The Asst. Registrar asked all of the candidates to wait till afternoon for the final result, giving a ray of hope to attend the final interview. Mean while one old person; an HR consultant, has gone for the presentation. When the other candidates were discussing their indifferent experience from the board members, they observed quiet unusual incident that within a period of 10 minutes the consultant HR, came out of the presentation hall and went out without even looking at us. His face was so much angered and irritated.

The Director came out of the board room and called the Asst. Registrar. After having three minutes discussion with the Director, the Asst. Registrar, took all of the candidates to the Cafeteria. He talked with us very enthusiastically and shared lot of information about Hyderabad and several tourist locations within the city limit, for visit. The interaction with Asst. Registrar had given better hope to all of three that they would be selected for the final interview on 9th.

After lunch he took us to the Office of Registrar. He paid us the travel expenses incurred. Prof. Ramarajan got 3613Rs, The IIM faculty got 3659Rs and the ICFAI faculty got 2900Rs. Soon after, he led us to the taxi stand and arranged a vehicle and driver to drop us in the Centre for Management, Banjara Hills. Meanwhile, the IIM faculty enquired about the result of the presentation. Having a smile and satirical reply he informed all of us that 'no one has selected in the presentation for the final interview.' The news became shocking to all of the candidates.

With anxiety, all of them asked the Asst. Registrar that as per the call letter, they booked their tickets on 10th August and till that day where they would lodge? The Asst. Registrar replied that 'see the interview has been an ongoing process.... just like you people, we have already interviewed 113 candidates in the last one month. No matter, you can stay at Banjara Hills, in the Centre for Management Hostel room as long as you want. Enjoy the rest of the days with some site-seeing.

Hurriedly, without looking at their face, he gave a big hand to the candidates and paved 'good bye.

'They further heard his direction to the taxi-driver that 'bring the other four candidates from Banjara Hills for after noon presentation, when you return.'

The car started moving... carrying the 'three unfortunates.'

Questions

1. Discuss the importance of unambiguous interview letter.
2. Discuss the institutional objectives of presentation and interaction.
3. Discuss the ethical stand of board members in the presentation and interaction.
4. Discuss the attitude of candidates on the presentation and interaction.
5. How far the institute is conscious about cost of interviews?
6. Discuss the importance of right HR practices that facilitate better administration?

Case 13

COMPETENCY MAPPING AND COMPENSATION MANAGEMENT

Prof. Uma Sreenivasan and Prof. Dholakia, both are Assistant Professors in Marketing Management in a leading business school, in Pune. Both have more than 20 years of experience in the field. Prof. Uma Sreenivasan has been working in the organisation last four years, and Prof. Dholakia was appointed recently. The fight between the two Assistant Professors started when Prof. Uma Sreenivasan came to know that her compensation package is very less compared to Prof. Dholakia. She observed a margin of 10000/Rs difference in her salary with that of Prof. Dholakia. She observed greater disparity of management decision in giving more compensation package to a person who has same experience and fewer qualifications, compared to her. She become very annoyed and lodged a grievance letter to the Director General (Management). When the Director General looked into the matter, he observed the same disparity. He called the Director of the institute for a confidential analysis and asked him to submit a report within one week. The relationship between the Director and Prof Uma Sreenivasan has not been congenial, since the day of her appointment. As per the discussion, the institute Director took up all the files of these two Assistant Professors and made a confidential analysis and prepared a report. He sent that report to the Director General within one week showing his own conclusion on the matter and for further proceeding. The Director General called a meeting of the Directors to discuss this issue for an open analysis. Some of the Directors in the meeting did not like Prof. Uma Sreenivasan and purposefully spoke against the decision for a pay hike to her. Since majority of the Directors went against the decision to hike her salary. After observing some discrepancy in the discussion, the Director General decided to go for second level analyses to get further details. He asked one of the senior HR Professor of the institute go for further analysis and asked him to report within three days. In addition to that he directed the HR Professor to go for student feedback also in this matter. As per the direction the HR Professor looked into the matter and found that the complaint lodged by Prof. Uma Sreenivasan is justifiable to a certain extend. Instead of coming to a conclusion himself he sent the report and feedback letter to the Director for further proceedings. The details of the report and the letter of HR Professor to the Director General are as follows.

Comparative Analysis if Two Assistant Professors

Areas	*Prof. Rakesh Dholakia*	*Prof. Uma Sreenivasan*	*Remarks*
Qualifications	B.Sc (Chemistry, Botany, Zoology) MBA Marketing) Pursuing Ph.D.	M.Phill, MBA (International Marketing) MA (History) B.Ed (English) BA (Politics) DJ & PRDHM & CT	The educational background of Prof. Uma Srinivasan indicates her involvement, orientation and keen interest in academic career to pursue Business Management and Service industry. Her educational qualification qualifications are higher compared to Prof. Dholakia.
Total years of experience	22 years in industry 2.3 years in academic	11 Years Advertising Organization 2 years Own Business 4.4 Years Education (Service industry)	Industrial experience is found more with Prof. Dholakia compared to Uma Srinivasan. Uma Srinivasan is having Own Business Management (OWM) experience.
Teaching Experience	**2.3 years**	**4.4 Years**	Prof. Dholakia's work experience in teaching to university and other educational centres are found limited (2 years) compared to Prof. Uma Srinivasan (4.4 years). Teaching exposure is found more with Uma Srinivasan compared to Prof. Dholakia.

Contd.

Organizations Served and Positions Held	2.3 years as **Visiting faculty/ Associate Professor** in Professional Tutorials Pioneer Institute of Management and Mahakal Institute of Management.	**Assistant Professor 3 Years** AMA International University and **1.3 Year** SIBACA experience as Assistant Professor.	The consistency and persistence of Prof. Uma Srinivasan to serve newly joined organizations is found stable compared to Prof. Dholakia. His profile indicates that within 2.3 years of academic life he switched over twice in his service to organization.
Roles Performed	General Knowledge Communication SkillsEnglish UsageMarketing Business EnvironmentStrategic Management Organizational Behavior	Business Communication Advertising and Sales Promotion Industrial Psychology Principles of Management International Marketing International RelationsEnglish UsageWorld HistoryPolitical Science and World Governance	Both, the Assistant Professors viz., Prof. Dholakia and Prof. Uma Srinivasan, are having the knowledge base of Business Communication and Marketing management.Prof. Dholakia is more specialized in the area of Strategic Marketing Management and Prof. Uma Srinivasan is in Advertising and Sales Promotion. These Professor's knowledge base in their core areas further to be tested as they have more industrial experience than teaching experience. How these Professors are good in communicating their specialized knowledge base to students are more important than having wider experience.
Feed Back of Students	**Good**	**Good/ Moderately Good**	Prof. Dholakia is good in teaching marketing management subject.Prof. Uma Srinivasan is good in teaching business communications subject and moderately good (average) in marketing management.
Contribution to Universities and Institutes	**Teaching** General Knowledge Communication SkillsEnglish UsageMarketing Business Environment Strategic Management Organizational BehaviorResearch Methodology	**Teaching** Business Communication Advertising and Sales Promotion Industrial Psychology Principles of Management International Marketing International Relations	In addition to the teaching assignment Prof. Uma Srinivasan has been engaged in many extra curricular activities which are directly contributing to personality development of students in SIBACA and SBS.While the contribution of Prof. Dholakia is limited to educational activities alone. Since his service started only from July onwards it is not right to make a judgment in this regard.

Contd.

Development Programs to institutes	No Information	7 day faculty initiation and orientation program in Malia, Philippines 2 days Oil Gas Corporate Communication Program 10 days Faculty Development Program in SIBAR Kondhwa. Organized many students development program to Abroad University and SIBACA. Talent displays, fashion shows, and communication skill programs are organized in SIBACA.	
Seminars and Workshops attended	No information.	Many Seminars and work shop attended	Exposure to Seminars and Workshop found more with Uma Srinivasan compared to Prof. Dholakia.
Industry/ Business Experience	22 Years worked in different industries within India	11 years worked in Multinational Advertising company abroad 2 years own Public Relation and Advertising Consulting Company.	Prof. Dholakia is found far experienced person in Marketing and Business Development.Prof. Uma Srinivasan is having well experience in international companies in the field of advertising (sales promotion) business communication.
Positions Held in Different Business Organizations	Manager (Marketing)- (Domestic Organizations)	Manager (Advertising and Sales Promotion) - (Abroad)	Both the Professors served in the industry and business organizations as Manager (Marketing) and claimed their contribution to profitability and efficiency.
Skills	Negotiation Communication Teaching Training	Inter Personal Relationship Negotiation . Communication Teaching Training Effort	Though these Professors are good in many skills they lack research aptitude. None of these Professors made any research publication during their academic or industrial career.

Contd.

Expected Future contribution	To SIBACA and SBS as Faculty Researcher Trainer to MDP Institutional Development	To SIBACA and SBS as Faculty Researcher Trainer to MDP Editor to Journals/ Publications Institutional Development	These Professors are expected to contribute many areas in their institutional service. Prof. Uma has shown their willingness to assist Prof. Dileep Kumar in his to stabilize SBS. (Refer the biodata)
Salary	19000/-	28000/-	High difference in the pay package of Prof. Dholakia and Prof. Uma sreenivasan in the same position and scale.

From 02-08-2005

Professor-HR
Ringad Business School
Pune.

To

The Director General
Rinagad Business School,
Sadasiv Peth
Pune

Respected Sir,

Sub: Compensation Package Revision of Prof. Uma Srinivasan

As per your direction I have made a comparative analysis of the profile and pay package of Prof. Uma Srinivasan with Prof. Dholakia. I have arrived at following remarks in this regard.

- The educational background of Prof. Uma Srinivasan indicates her involvement, orientation and keen interest in academic career to pursue Business Management and Service industry. The educational qualifications of Prof. Uma Srinivasan is higher compared to Prof. Dholakia.
- Industrial experience is found more with Prof. Dholakia compared to Uma Srinivasan

- Uma Srinivasan has Own Business Management (OWM) experience.
- Prof. Dholakia's work experience in teaching to university and other educational centres are found limited (2 years) compared to Prof. Uma Srinivasan (4.4 years).
- Teaching exposure is found more with Uma Srinivasan compared to Prof. Dholakia.
- The consistency and persistence of Prof. Uma Srinivasan to serve newly joined organizations is found stable compared to Prof. Dholakia. His profile indicates that within 2.3 years of academic life he switched over twice in his service to different organizations.
- Both, the Assistant Professors viz., Prof. Dholakia and Prof. Uma Srinivasan, are having the knowledge base of Business Communication and Marketing management.
- Prof. Dholakia is more specialized in the area of Strategic Marketing Management and Prof. Uma Srinivasan is in Advertising and Sales Promotion.
- The Professor's knowledge base in the core areas is further to be tested as they have more industrial experience than teaching experience. Communicating their specialized knowledge base to students is more important than having wider experience.
- Prof. Dholakia is good in teaching marketing management subject.
- Prof. Uma Srinivasan is excellent in teaching business communications and allied subjects and moderately good in marketing management.
- In addition to the teaching assignment Prof. Uma Srinivasan has been engaged in many extra curricular activities, which directly contributes to the personality development of the students.

- The contribution of Prof. Dholakia is limited to educational activities alone. Since, his service started only from July onwards, it is not right to make any judgment in this regard.
- Exposure to Seminars and Workshop found more with Uma Srinivasan compared to Prof. Dholakia.
- Prof. Dholakia is found far more experienced person in Marketing and Business Development.
- Prof. Uma Srinivasan has good experience in international companies in the field of advertising (sales promotion) business communication.
- Both the Professors served in the industry and business organizations as Manager (Marketing) and claimed their contribution to profitability and efficiency.
- Though these Professors are good in many skills they lack research aptitude. None of these Professors had any research publication during their academic or industrial career.
- These Professors are expected to contribute in many areas in their institutional service.

Remarks

- Both Professors are good in their respective areas (Marketing Management and Business Communication)
- The experience of Prof. Dholakia is outstanding in marketing management.
- The experience of Prof. Uma in Business is communication is excellent.
- There is compensation variation between the two Assistant Professors.
- An additional payment to Prof. Uma Srinivasan is justifiable, based on her qualification experience & contribution.
- The compensation of Prof. Uma Srinivasan can be raised, with two periodical frame work. The first hike within 6

months and the second will in the 7th month by observing her contribution at work.

Let, me submit these report for your kind perusal and further proceedings.

Thanking you

Yours faithfully

HR Professor–

RBS

Case Continues

The Director General has gone through the report and has taken an immediate decision to hike her salary by 5000/Rs for the coming 6 months and the remaining in the following period. He sent a letter to the President of the organisation, showing these details and recommending for an immediate hike. Soon after the Director General sent a show cause notice to the existing Director within one week, for dilution of facts and figures.

Questions

1. Do you feel there is any disparity in compensation package?
2. Map the competence of both Professors and go for job evaluation?
3. To what extent the authority of the Director is accountable to the subordinates?
4. How do you relate this incident with the employee motivation?
5. How the leadership of the organisation is trust worthy?
6. Do you fee that this organisation has any reward and promotion policy?
7. How does organizational politics affect the promotions and advancement?
8. Which Assistant Professor is suitable to teach in a Post Graduate-MBA program?
9. Differentiate the leadership of the Director General and the Director of the institute?

Case 14

NEGOTIATION AND SETTLEMENT

Orion Bank is one of the premier cooperative banks in Kerala. The financial performance of the company and the customer's satisfaction is very high. It has got better acceptance in Kerala community. Mr. Radha Raman was the Manager of Orion Bank, its head office situated in Cochin. Actually the bank is a model for other cooperative bank with its minimum employees providing maximum service to their customers.

As and when the business of the bank increases the employees in the organisation faced with acute job difficulty and job stress. The Manger of a bank is flooded every day with immense responsibilities and customer grievances especially complaint against cashiers, lack of cleanliness, delay in timing and also attending to important customers send by Board of Directors etc. More over the Board of Directors had not given adequate power and responsibilities to thier managers to take action independently since the bank is cooperative one. Fed up with the lack of authority and day today problems in handling bank transactions and customers, the earlier manager resigned from his position.

The Board of Directors offered the position to Mr. Thomas, the Assistant Manager. He declined the offer saying that he is not interested in the position. Actually, his interest lies more on his return of investment. He knows that the position required more authority and responsibilities to handle the function effectively. More than that the position requires responsibilities plunged with high risk. The office manager's who are engaged with is more responsible with work day to day assignments expect more compensation package and fringe benefits. As such no increment and additional amount has been offered by the Board of Directors Mr. Thomas, the Assistant Manager denied the offer.

The Board of Director then interviewed about 15 managers who would like to switch over from their existing banks. The demands of the prospective managers were so huge that the Board of Directors couldn't accommodate their demands. They decided to accommodate the least demanded person on the vacant position and selected a bank manager of other bank, by changing the existing wage agreement policy, to accommodate him.

More over, a person with long experience, in managing urban cooperative banks has been appointed as the GM very recently. The new GM has been given a salary of Rs. 40000/m plus free furnished housing with an official car for his mobility.

The Office Manager Mr. Vikram is very much frustrated with these changes. He has torpedoed the recently concluded wage agreement by influencing the office bearers of the union although 90% of employee signed the agreement.

Mr. Thomas approached the consultant who was mediating the settlement to recommend the Board of Directors for a raise of Rs. 4000/-m plus free housing for him as the new GM has been given a salary of Rs. 40000/m plus free furnished housing with an official car for his mobility and other allowances. He has compared all the new allowances which are allocated for the new GM with other employees.

Questions

1. Discuss the case with negotiation and settlement concept.
2. Discuss the role of Board of Directors power and authority over the case.
3. How you justify the hike of Mr. Thomas if any required?
4. Discuss the labour dynamics and employee perception?

CASE 15

RESIGNATION OR TERMINATION

KC School of Management and Sciences (KSCMS) was established in 1994 to impart excellent quality higher education in the areas of management and sciences. KCMS offers undergraduates and post graduate programmes ranging from business management and information technology to social work, psychology, tourism, hotel management, arts and humanities. KCMS currently offers programs of Master of Business Administration (MBA), Master of Computer Applications (MCA), Master of Tourism Administration (MTA), Master of Social Work (MSW), All India Management Association's two year Post Graduate Diploma in Business Management (PGDM) and Post Graduate Diploma in Information Technology Management (PGDITM), Bachelor in Business Management (BBM), Bachelor in Computer Applications (BCA) and Bachelor in Hotel Management (BHM) courses.

Mr. Debojith Mukharjee is the CEO of KC School of Management and Sciences. He is an MBA graduate from XLRI and did his Engineering from IIT, Kharagpur. He is a person having well reputation for imparting value education to people in West Bengal. He has written many books and has number of publications in national and international journals. Since he has to undertake issues related to institutional expansion he has decided to appoint an administrator who has sound experience in teaching and management. More over, he has to settle down some campus issues in one of the institute's regional centre, which started recently and are facing more severe student level and administrative problems.

He appointed Mr. Bharth Verma as the Associate Dean of the campus. Verma has 30 years of experience in teaching English literature and he has done one master programme in Business Management. His experience in teaching business Management is very limited. Still Mr. Mukharjee appointed him as the dean of the campus considering experience in administration as stop gap arrangement. There is a good number of senior faculty members who are experienced enough to take up the responsibilities of Associate Dean. But Mr. Mukharjee insisted an external person who can intervene in these problems objectively.

Mr. Verma started his work by getting close with a few faculty members in the institution and gets to know the people who may create barrier in his journey towards greater power and position in the institution. He took the confidence of Mr. Mukharjee the CEO of KC School of Management and Sciences, through his cleverness. Gradually, Mr. Verma turned up as a "terror figure' in the campus. Every body started feeling insecure on his administrative decisions. He terminated many administrative staff members. Those who do not follow his decision have to face personal problems by Mr. Verma.

Soon after he controlled all the administrative staff under him, he decided to act up on the faculty members. He reported false information on certain faculty members, who have been working in this institute for a long period to build up the institute as one of the best management schools in West Bengal. Mr. Mukharjee started trusting Mr. Verma's report and took some stringent steps to clear the system for betterment. He asked a few excellent faculty members to resign from the institute as remedial measures to solve the students and administrative issues. Among which Dr. Kiran Rai was also included. Dr. Rai, who's having 28 years of educational experience in management education and meritorious track record in his career was asked to leave the organisation based on his some indecent comments on students and better hold on students in their decision making.

He was working in the institute as Chief Programme Officer-PGDM programme for the past 2 and half years. He was handling this programme meticulously for the past 2 and a half years, even with its autonomous status, and the programme was getting more acceptances among students' in better placements.

The decision of Mr. Mukharjee was a shock to Dr. Rai. He came to know from some body in the institute that, his dismissal from the service is due to the pressure of Mr. Bharth Verma, that to block him from getting into high position in the organisation. Mr. Bharth Verma, asked Dr. Rai to 'resign' from the position that to avoid his 'termination' from the service. Instead of accepting the administrative decision Dr. Rai sent a letter to the CEO indicating his lack of willingness to accept the allegations against him by Mr. Verma and requested him to offer a termination letter from his side. But the CEO did not reply his letter seeking termination from the service. The CEO called Dr. Rai, in his cabin and explained the details given by Mr. Verma. The CEO asked him to accept the self resignation to avoid termination from the institute based on the indecent remarks. Mr. Verma was also present in that last meeting. Mr. Dr. Rai didn't reply anything to the CEO or Mr. Verma and silently moved out of CEO's cabin.

By reaching home he sent a mail to the CEO in his e-mail.

From 22-05-04
(Midnapur)

Dr. Kiran Rai
Professor-Management Studies
KC School of Management
Midnapur, West Bengal

To

Mr. Debojith Mukharjee (CEO)
KC School of Management and Sciences
Midnapur, West Bengal

Dear Sir,

Sub : Non-Receipt of Termination Letter
Ref : The discussion on 22-05-04 the resignation from Service

Hope this mail finds with you in the best of health and spirits. This letter is for your kind perusal and favorable consideration.

Before I extend any demand, let me recollect all the good works, which I have done to build up credibility to your academic institution.

When I joined your organisation, I saw an unprofessional culture over there.

- Students come and go at any time,
- Students can take leave as per their choice.
- Students, wearing slippers.
- Lot of leisure
- Lot of indecent behaviour
- Students with arrogant attitude
- Faculty members come and go at any time,
- Students felt cent-percent dissatisfaction on management and faculty members
- Lack of curriculum
- Dissatisfied faculty members
- Dissatisfaction of parents
- No training for students
- No classes for students
- No industrial visit
- No corporate interaction
- No norms and regulations
- No attendance system
- No administrator
- The staff members sit idle and are irresponsible in their job

- Movement of vehicles in accordance with the staff members choices
- No value orientation

And many more...!!!!

To bring the professionalism to the campus, let me share what I contributed during last few years.

- Introduced disciplinary actions.
- Introduced Yoga and Meditation.
- Introduced uniform system within the campus.
- Introduced 100% attendance management system.
- Working hours changed from 10-4 to 7.30-8.30 (so that students won't get enough time to go to 'Booze' up and engage in 'love affairs').
- No holiday (Including Sunday).
- Controlled alcohol intake within the hostel.
- New Curriculum designed with more number of core papers, soft papers and training programmes.
- The curriculum converted into credit and trimester system.
- Introduced best faculty members from other states that invite student's satisfaction.
- Brought more permanent faculty members to the campus.
- Introduced more work-assignment system (reduced the leisure)
- Introduced "corporate monitoring-students presentations" on every afternoon.
- Introduce "Economic Times" paper-(The English business news paper on their doors in every morning)
- Introduce "Business World" Subscription.
- Conducted regular business quiz competition to develop business awareness to students.
- Compulsory news paper reading and reading journals.

- Introduced 'case study' approach in the campus.
- Introduced SPSS training for students.
- Conducted a research on KC book fair.
- Invited parent support in the implementation of a rigorous curriculum.
- Prepared the schedule of exams and coordinated well.
- Giving students feed back to the parents frequently
- Introduced Foreign language–French with the collaboration of Alliance Francaise
- Conducted many corporate interaction–guest lectures
- Arranged industrial visit for the students
- Organised "QUALITE"–a Two Day National Workshop on 'Quality Management System' with trainers from BHEL New Delhi.
- Organised "Budget Analysis" one-day seminar on National Budget 2007 with more than 100 participants.
- Actively involved in the AICTE inspection process.
- Prepared the PGDM Academic structure and syllabus to regional campus.
- Spent 24 hours with the students to groom them towards better professional being.
- Provided individual and group counselling to resolve the personal problems
- Provided career counseling
- Acted as a mentor and coach to the students and faculty members
- Finalized the students 12 page campus "News Letter"
- Arranged a new hostel to the boys
- Controlled unnecessary vehicle movement
- Controlled unnecessary electricity usage
- The administration become so rigid to make the system effective

- Organised and Engaged in the admission process
- Brought 60 students from North India for PGDM programme
- Prepared the prospectus of KSCSM-PGDM 2007 programme

I am aware of the change in administration that happened recently. I believe that what ever I have done is for the absolute control and maintenance of campus discipline. I followed the instructions of Mr. Varma and the CEO. The action you have taken is ignoring my contributions to institute and the report which is given by the Associate Dean on my indecent comments. Ever shall I use any indecent words against my students and never shall I open my ears to indecent languages, as a teacher, in the students grooming process. It's my strong conviction that a teacher has the full authority to understand students, scold them and direct them to lead a better social and professional life, considering their growth and development.

The steps I have taken to turn around the campus are to produce best business professionals from KSCSM. But alas, after turning around the campus the management doesn't want my service. You went on with student's plea and the report from the Associate Dean.

No matter. World is round. For a PhD holder with 28 years of experience, high competency, self-confidence, and value orientation, it won't be difficult to get a 'work with joy.'

Many..many..thanks for whatever the support you rendered me till date.

Let me come to the point.

All along, I have been waiting for your termination letter, that in continuation with the discussion in the presence of Mr. Varma, Associate Dean KSCSM Institutions, regarding the 'termination' of my service as Chief Programme Officer, KSCSM. I have vacated your rented building within two days, since you asked me to leave the campus within one week 'with grace.' I have given my laptop, laptop-bag, Internet card, Pen drive and other materials that I used for effective functional dissemination, to Mr. Abraham, Administrative Officer, KCSM Institutions, Midnapur. I am ready to clear all the dues that I incurred to the institute, as per your intimation.

As per the clause 5, of appointment letter (this appointment is terminable by one month's notice on either side or payment of remuneration in lieu of notice) of the appointment order by KCM Foundation, you are liable to *pay my one month salary,* since you terminated my service, unilaterally, from KCSM Institutions.

Since I don't want to resign my post, as I expect your 'termination letter' at the earliest to my home address.

May GOD bless you in your entire endeavour.... Luciax Lux Vestra.

Thanking you

Yours faithfully

Dr. Kiran Rai

"Neither CEO nor the Associate Dean replied his mail"

Discussion Questions

1. Discuss the role of organisational politics in understanding human behaviour at work.
2. How can you evaluate the role of leadership in organisation?
3. If you would be in the position of CEO, what decisions and actions you would take?
4. How far loyalty and trust of members affected by the incidents?
5. Would you prefer resignation considering the practical step?
6. How far organisational change affects culture of the organisation?
7. When report and contributions comes to your table which one you prefer?

Case 16

INNOVATIVE HR

AICA Pharmaceutical Pvt. Ltd is a Multi National Pharmaceutical Company which started its business operations in India during 2004. The company products got better appreciation from the Northern part of India. The better business opportunities across Northern states have leaded the management to expand its operations to Southern part of India. The CEO has given direction to the Vice President HR to prepare a manpower and recruitment plan which leads to the satisfaction of an employee and ensure retention.

The Vice President HR has called a meeting and directed the HR members to go ahead with an innovative HR practice that ensure new errant in multi functional areas to start their performance with a differential induction program. The Vice President HR is very particular about the innovative HR Practice in manpower planning, recruitment, selection and induction. The Vice President HR further instructed their HR team members to follow an employee with an employee friendly hiring practices. The HR team has given a different add which details about the recruitment process in a leading newspapers of the country.

The HR department got around 600 applications. The initial task of HR department was to analyze the suitability of the candidates to the positions which are to be filled up. All applications were treated in a strict vigilance. The information about the recruitment and selection process has kept strict confidential. Different from common HR practice the company has sent call letters to each applicant detailing the company information, products, services, process, markets, future plans, names of key manager etc. It has been keenly taken care by the HR department that the new applicants should feel entire process of selection as informal. Further they insist that the candidates should feel relaxed and open up their interest aspiration towards their job without having any fear or hesitation. There was an interactive session and the candidates found themselves at ease in the interview. The HR department heard the process as "the company follows better treatment from the candidates".

ALCA PHARMACEUTICAL PVT LTD

AlCA Pharmaceutical Pvt Ltd is a multinational company having factories in USA and Europe is ranked among the top ten Pharmaceutical companies world wide. The company needs highly energetic and motivated individual who dare to dreamand learn to achieve. If you feels you are one among them, read this message:

We Require

SALES EXECUTIVES

(Southern Region)

Qualifications and Background–

- Post Graduation with Academic Excellence
- Experience in Sales/Related Areas Five Years
- Passion to take Challenging Assignments
- Grow with Company

If you qualify call up +91 9881000100 and fix up a meeting or you may send your resume to

abc@alikeco.com

Your Communication is Confidential

The company short listed 20 people from the interview process. Those who were short-listed by the company received offer letter and invited for a get together with other sales team and the Vice President of HR in the company resort. Candidates were short listed and those who received offer letter were in a surprise since the offer was delivered at their doorstep by an important role holder, by the Manager HR.

The Manger HR, spend some time with the candidate's family members also to clarify their doubts pertaining to the functional responsibilities, compensation package, perks and incentives, career growth etc. Further to that, during the get together, the Vice President HR interacted with all the 20 short listed candidates personally. The Vice President HR enquired about the family members of the candidates and their status. He briefed the candidates about the career growth that in tune with the company growth. He had given one week time to each employee to think, whether they were ready to join the company.

It was surprised to see that all the 20 employees have decided to join the company on the stipulated date. The new entrant joins, s/he has many novelties, a welcome letter, an updated manual (Organisation, Departments, Policies, Procedures, Rules, Regulations, Forms), a cabin/work station, fully furnished, with meticulous detailing and above all a role holder to receive her/him at the gate. The HR department has arranged warm welcome to the new entrant.

The HR manager has given his personal welcome which is followed by induction programme, specially designed to give more inputs to the roles and responsibilities to the new sales executives. The senior manager's of sales are also present there to clarify their doubts pertaining to operational activities. The sales executives have obtained detailed information about the products, the price of products, distribution locations, topographical awareness and special training on higher level selling skills. All the grievances of the new sales executives are better handled by the HR managers with due care and support. Thus within a period of thirty days the new entrant develops functional proficiency in all spheres of the organisation. The new sales executives are thus fine tuned with the family culture promoted by the company, functions and roles and responsibilities, that to excel towards their work with more commitment and dedication.

It was reported by the HR department that the new sales executive started liking the company much faster when compared to other employees.

Questions

1. Comment o the innovative HR practice followed by the company?
2. Do you feel that attraction of employee's would be made possible through innovative HR practices?
3. Justify upon the leader's role in bringing innovative HR practices.
4. How do the innovative HR practices induce organizational culture and motivation?
5. How far Induction Programs play effective role in functional orientation and values. Comment.

CASE 17

INNOVATIVE WELFARE

Trident Aeronautical Ltd (TAL) is a premier Private Sector undertaking of South East Asia, with 19 production/overhaul/service division and 6 co-located R&D centers across the country. TAL's spectrum of expertise encompasses hi-tech programmes, involving a number of state-of-art technology, design, development, manufacture, repair, overhaul, and upgrade of Aircraft, Helicopters, Aero-engines, Industrial and marine gas turbines, Accessories, Avionics, and systems and Structural components, for satellite and launch vehicles. Trident Aeronautical Ltd (TAL) is a progressive private ltd company located in the Nashik, Maharashtra.

The company is well aware of the importance of retention of their talented employees to retain their business growth and development. The HR and IR department of the company takes care of their employee's interest so as to retain their motivational level. As a part of their retention policy the company provides various innovative welfare provisions to their employees and also extended wider benefit to them. All the benefits would be made available to its employees and some to their families. The area (types of benefits) was mind boggling:

(a) Monthly get together along with the employees

(b) Personal development

(c) Personal Health Care

(d) Club membership

(e) Yearly vacation along with families
(f) Purchase of Managerial & Technical books
(g) Recreation, other then sports
(h) Subscription to professional Journals
(i) Transportation facilities for employee's
(j) Purchase of Musical Instruments
(k) Awards and gifts for long service employees. 5 yrs, 10 yrs, 20 and 30 yrs etc.,
(l) Flexi-time
(m) Yoga & Spiritual courses
(n) Suggestion scheme- award for the best suggestions
(o) Medical Reimbursement
(p) Send greeting card for birthdays
(q) Social & Village Activities
(r) Coverage of employees under some insurance policies
(s) Photography Courses
(t) Career Counselling
(u) For stay in Tourist Hotels rum by Central/State Government
(v) Advancement training at the cost of company
(w) Studies in Medicine, engineering, Architecture, Accountancy, Management (esp. for dependents)
(x) Soft loans free of interest
(y) Languages Courses.
(z) Best attendance awards
(aa) Routine health check up
(bb) Pay supplements (Compensation for non working periods)

The employees had to first spend and thereafter claim reimbursement "THIS IS UNIQUE". In certain areas like Medical Reimbursement, employees who had retired were also eligible, and for them the reimbursement was as high as 80%.

The good health of the employee is in the best interest of the Company. Therefore the activities of the Medical Department, although intended to serve first the concerns of the Company, also act to protect employee health. The Company maintains medical facilities for the use of employees in the Company premises. Registered nurses are on duty from 8:30 A.M. to 4:30 P.M. From 5:00 P.M. to 1:00 A.M., a registered nurse is on duty for the employees who are assigned to the evening and night shifts.

Group Mediclaim Policy of the company covers employees' health at a reasonable cost and gives the organisation more competitive edge. The company also allowed the retired employees to be covered by its Group Mediclaim Policy, thus they stood covered till death. This was a great boon since it is at this age that persons fall sick and they have to spend a considerable amount to pay their medical bills. Assistance is available to supervisors, through Medical Department, in resolving problems of work performance and absenteeism when the probable causes are health, emotional disorder, and alcoholism or drug abuse.

What a facility, of free medical cover, even after retirement. So the employees continued to be a part of Trident Aeronautical Ltd (TAL) till death took away their embodiment.

Questions

1. Critically evaluate the relevance of welfare provisions in this company?
2. Do you believe that the welfare provisions can retain the talented employees for a long period?
3. Critically evaluate the importance of welfare provisions under new labour policy.
4. How you perceive this opinion "Welfare Measures doesn't have any role among Knowledge Workers".

Case 18

VRS AND WOMEN EMPLOYEES

Radha working as Assistant Manager and Malini working as Stenographers in the Camoflag Fertilizers and Chemicals Ltd., a Public Ltd Company in Maharashtra. The organization has decided to announce VRS to curb the financial outlay incurred in the past decades. The news about VRS spread rapidly all over the organization. Since, Malini and Radha work in the same department they get an opportunity to discuss their own opinion and attitude towards VRS and employment

Radha : Have you heard about implementing VRS in our company?

Malilni : Yes, I have.

Radha : Do you have any decision to opt?

Malini : No I don't have.

Radha : Why?

Malini : I need my job to support my family and myself.

Radha : What I heard is that the compensation package is good enough to opt for VRS. But there is high uncertainty about VRS.

Malini : Yes it is true.

Radha : I asked you this why because you have to travel a long distance to come over here to do your work everyday. Your salary is not that in commensurate with your work and effort. If you had worked in a private firm you would have get better salary.

Malini : In your case, it may be true. But to me it is not that easy what we see externally. Many qualified hands exist outside to get employment. More over they are ready to work under low salary. The management will opt only those individuals who opt low compensation packages for their work. A state, where there is huge educated unemployed youth, it is difficult to find a job to survive. I feel, it will be a good decision that not to opt VRS at this juncture. It is true that I have to travel a long distance to do my work. No matter, I will continue the same. After all, my job is permanent. I don't want to remain as an educated unemployed by opting VRS.

Radha : See after downsizing and disinvestments policy we don't know where we would be and what will be our position. There are chances of distant transfers, delayed promotions, reduction in compensation packages, down gradation etc. All along we have been suffering the bully attitude of senior members. Here we are almost working as salves. Every day we have tension and anxiety to interact with these bossy people. Their attitude becomes more bullying after the introduction of VRS and disinvestments policies. Better we utilize this opportunity and leave the job.

Malini : Yes, the attitude of senior members may be bullying. But to live, we should get an income, for that we have to continue the job, some how. You know that still I live in a rented house. The construction of our house is in the midway. I have to repay several loans that were taken so far for my house. We are struggling to fulfill the requirements the month. See whatever it may happen; I am not going to loose my job and opt for VRS whatever might be the challenge.

Radha : Your decision considering your family affairs may be correct. But if you are transferred to any distant place, what would you do? How can you support your family members? Then in such case, your husband has to look after your family and the situation is much more complicated.

Malini : Ha..., its true, there may be chances of down gradation or transfers. But my husband is much cooperative. As you know he is very simple and highly supportive to me to continue this job. We realized that without money it is impossible to maintain lower middle class family. If I am transferred he will surely support me.

Radha : Any way I will opt VRS. I am fed up with this organization. I don't know how I had spent 22 years in this organization. It's a great opportunity to escape from this organization. It's a great relief from the 'bossy egos' and 'formal relations'. I feel that majority of managers in this organization know only to command their subordinates than try to do some thing independently. They want to hide their incompetence some how.

Malini : Any way you have better pay and better economic status. Your job may not make any difference in the economic stability of your family. But I cannot agree with your justification that simply because of bossy attitude of management, you opt for VRS.

Radha : Yes, it is true. Just like you I too am traveling long distance to continue this job. After all this job is only for namesake. I took this job not because of my own interest, but because of my parents. As in your case, I don't have to depend on my job to maintain my family. My husband has a good job in ICICI bank and is earning well. The purpose of the maintenance of this job is simply to get social status. Remember, we cannot tell others that here we are living just like a slave. Some how, I prefer to stop this affair some where. As the job doesn't have any value for me and for the management, what for should I continue in this organization. Where there is pleasure in work and contribution, there I should be. So long, as a mother and grand mother, I couldn't perform my responsibilities towards my children and grand children. By opting VRS at least I can serve them in the remaining years and derive satisfaction out of it. Here no one needs my service.

Malini : That's what I told you that my preferences are different from your preferences. Go on with your decision as it has importance in your life.

Questions

1. What are the anxieties that associated with VRS among employees?
2. How is the decision making closely related to the needs and wants?
3. How do the employees perceive the leadership of the organization?
4. Do you believe that work is primary to employees? Comment.
5. How does external environment affect the decision making of women employees?
6. Which 'theory of motivation' related to this case study?
7. How does need theory related to this case study?
8. How does the work value related to decision making?
9. What type of organizational culture does the organization have now?
10. What is the style of management?

Case 19

ROLE OF HR CONSULTANT

Gilma Software Ltd is a leading provider of PDF manipulation and printing tools for cross platform operating systems. Launched in September 2000, Traction Software Ltd remains unique in the PDF industry by offering innovative and useful tools to all types of users, Traction Software is one of few companies that offer a wide range of software tools for Windows, Macintosh, Linux & AIX. Gilma Software has built a substantial market presence with thousands of customers, including Fortune and Global 500 organizations in the legal & law services, financial/banking services, government industries, pharmaceutical, manufacturing, healthcare and education.

The company has more than 100 employees and majority of them belong to knowledge worker category. The company met with a problem in Communicative English with their knowledge workers, which is highly essential in bringing better project from abroad. The MD of the company called for a meeting with the HR departmental heads and discussed some innovative plans to meet the challenges. All along company approaches Corporate Training firms to do the management development programmes across various topics. Since the HR department experimented with all types of training methodologies with various corporate training groups, they find it difficult to tackle the issue. Finally the HR department approached expert management consultant's opinion regarding the same difficulty.

The HR department identified one of the leading Management Consultant and Training Firm in Bangalore to tackle the issues related to Communicative English. "The Metrics" is an Expert Management Consultant, Training Firm, Corporate Training body, Research Firm, teaching body and Counseling Firm providing Corporate Training, Counseling, Consultancy Services and Online Counseling, consisting of a pool of Management Consultants and Trainers having an experience of 15-20 years in their respective core competency areas. The Metrics undertakes management consultancy projects and corporate training programs and provides total management solutions. The Metrics department suggested a low cost model for a long period of two years involving teachers from the reputed schools in the city who are already part of the consulting firm in the training and development programmes instead of the so called corporate trainers for whom the company has to pay a lump sum amount and facilities to impart the training programmes.

The top management team including MD and GM-HR formed a task group with the Expert Management Consultant to implement a long term training and development programme which is cost effective and give maximum return of investment. They set 3 phases of Executive Development Programmes (EDPs) spread over two years with a structured follow-up and additional inputs between the phases.

The first phase consists of beginner's module. The second phase consists of development module and the third phase consists of exposure module. It is mandatory for the employees to attend this programme. One hour from their day to day work is allocated for the training and development programme. The employees are ready to spend their one hour to improve their proficiency in Communicative English. The number of hours available for interaction was high and it also provided the participants and faculty to 'socialise' in an informal setting, which was again a "high value" addition A batch of 30 was trained in separate timings. The trainer encouraged informal interactions across the session to get maximum participation from the members. Being a high profile programme, most of the officials from HR and also other role holders in the organisation attended the programme, to add value by meaningful interactions. The CEO joined all of them for few days as mark of encouragement. The course contents, methodology, processes and other interactional deliverables were mirrored 3-tier EDP's. Latter-on based on dialogue; modifications were carried-out to meet specific firm requirements also. The training consists of modules based on specific needs, including: English grammar fundamentals and common stumbling blocks, pronunciation, intonation, avoiding stuffy language, wordy or convoluted writing, jargon and clichés, recognizing the influence of the 'mother tongue', common 'Indianisms' and tips to avoid them, American and British English considerations etc that facilitate employees to realize the importance of English language in business. The day sessions were made very intensive often using the case study and business simulation methods, games, sports and lighter topics like music etc. The Quality of the programme was kept very high so that the students (employees) had plenty to gain. Language consultant conducts an individual interview with each trainee and gives feedback based on the result of training effectiveness on continuous basis. Participants who attended the programme rated it very high on the learning curve.

In a period of two years every employee in the organisation had undergone the Communicative English training course. It has been reported by the MD in a get together that the company turnover has increased considerably and that they can think of giving more dividend to employees this year. Supporting the result of effective training and consultation, the HR department has reported to the MD that more over the company has observe low level attrition in the last two years, which is a remarkable achievement. The motivation level of employee has increased and started thinking about long-term plan. To add to the positive result the company has decided to send more number of performers to aboard with enriched job there by to get more projects and business to company. Company appreciates the role of consultant in HR and Business solutions. The CEO of the company observed that "We don't have to send our employees to prestigious Business Schools for such training. This is the model India required for better organisational performance and growth.

Questions

1. Substantiate the role of consultants in providing solutions to business.
2. Discuss the role of HR managers as consultants and strategic partners than passive spectators of organisational issues.
3. Discuss the role of consultant in meeting budget objectives towards deliverables.
4. Constant monitoring and continuous evaluation are the pre-requisites for effective training. Discuss.
5. How did the design of the training programme helped in better participation among members?

Case 20

LEADERSHIP AND CULTURE

Softest Solutions Limited (SSL) is one of the software solution provider firms in the field of Human Resources, in India having 20 branches in and across the nation for over 15 years. The firm is well known in the circle for upholding human practices and keep follows friendly HR policy across the departments within the firm without bringing in levels, roles and positions for human connect. The staffs in the firms can freely interact with each other beyond their functional roles and the firm believes in collaborative business practices.

Mr. Rithin Nair is an efficient software marketing manager in Ingrad Micro Solution Pvt Ltd - a software firm in Calcutta. He and his children were staying in Calcutta for the past 10 years. Having the frequent request from his wife and other family members and considering the children better education he has decided to shift from Calcutta to Bangalore. He has applied in Softest Solutions Limited (SSL) in Bangalore for the post of Sr. Marketing Professional. The HR of the company refer the profile of Mr. Rithin Nair to CEO for the final approval interview process. The CEO also impressed with the profile and accomplishments of Mr. Rithin Nair and had given green signal for further processing. The HR department had an informal telephonic interaction with Mr. Rithin Nair to understand the demand of Mr. Rithin Nair. The demands of Mr. Rithin Nair were acceptable to the firm. He had called for an interaction with HR and CEO within 15 days on a mutually convenient date.

The interaction with HR and CEO was so informal that Mr. Rithin Nair like the culture of the company and the approach of CEO very much. He took the decision to relocate to Bangalore by serving the notice period of 30 days. Many offers were made by the firm to Mr. Rithin Nair. The firm agreed to pay for all the costs viz. travel and stay for self, wife and two kids from Calcutta to Bangalore and back, to get a feel of the place, transportation cost of all personal effects, an assignment for his wife, schooling for the kids all in house. He had to just walk-in to Bangalore with empty hands and there was a pent house reserved for him.

Mean while the CEO of the company has a visit to Calcutta for an official purpose. During his visit, the CEO took an initiative to interact with him in Calcutta and had breakfast so that they could enhance their relationship. The CEO in his very first meet put his hand around and also embraced him, just like two friends. Mr. Rithin Nair thought well about the CEO of the Softest Solutions Limited (SSL) as a person with a substance. They talked for an hour on all mutually interesting topics. The CEO concluded the meeting by saying CMCL and Goa "Needs You"

Mr. Rithin Nair shifted from Calcutta to Bangalore within the notice period itself, when the firm was ready to compensate his salary lose with the last employer. He started working with Softest Solutions Limited (SSL). He got better acceptance in the field as Bangalore is Silcon Valley for software business. The day of further reckoning arrives, SM arrives in Bangalre and it is a Sunday. The company had arranged a get together in Bangalore inviting many employees across the branches. The CEO with his eagle eyes spots Mr. Nithin Nair and gives him a place of honour and CEO had given an better appreciation and recognition to his credential and accomplishments in the firm in period of three months itself. Mr. Nithin Nair got wondered about CEOs knowledge about his contributions and accomplishments. More over he enquired about the children education and comfort of family members in Bangalore.

And there are many such instances where the CEO has gone miles to provide personal comfort and induce the culture of the organisation to Mr. Nithin Nair. He patted himself for the right decision that he had taken, to translocate from Calcutta to Bangalore. Mr. Nair proudly says this is the culture; all staffs are provided with benefits galore ...why should one leave Softest Solutions Limited (SSL) and that too with the personal touch of the CEO.

Questions

1. Describe the role of CEO as a business leader.
2. Discuss the role of CEOs in the creation and maintenance of organizational culture.
3. Do you believe that personal comfort with the organisation is an important factor in employee satisfaction?
4. How the culture of organisation influence employee motivation.
5. Analyze the leadership traits of CEO?
6. Discuss the case in detail with Hertzberg's two factor theory?

CASE 21

ME, MYSELF AND WORK CULTURE

The Reality

I am Joseph, working as foremen in Atles Swipco a Public Ltd Company, at Cochin, Kerala. I am have 25 years of experience in this organization. Our family settled at Kakkanad, hardly ten kilometers away from the industry. I have two children and my wife is a homemaker. I am a graduate and my wife has only secondary qualification. My children are studying in colleges at Pune. Many times, I used to think about my organisation and myself, during my leisure hours. The long twenty-five long years I have lot of questions in my mind. How I feel about me, my work, the history of organisation.... about the management and work culture. Whenever I tried to recollect all these points, every time, people around my family, peers or work disturbed, my sincere effort to think on all these aspects.

This year is my 25th year. I decided to recollect all my experience with this organisation. Having determined I kept myself away from all of the disturbances of life and started thinking of my past 25 years work life. As usual, I started to make a close scrutiny about my organization within myself.

To me, the culture of my organization is a way of life of all the employees and employers. The work values that the employee feels from his experience viz., while he is engaged in his functional and nonfunctional activities as a member of organization. I feel that the culture of organization is created developed and maintained by several factors. All such factors equally influenced and contributed in the formation of the way of life and interaction within the organization. Such factors include the employees, the employers, the trade unions, government and many such significant groups that exert influence upon the policy level and behavioral level. The values of the organizations are developed by the constant interaction and inter relation between all those factors mentioned above. The behaviour of employees and employers is actually the manifestation of the cultural practices of organizations. A healthy interaction between management and workers can be considered as the behavioral manifestation of cultural prevalence and affiliation to one kind of style of management, which is widely held, and shared by the organizational members.

I agree with the self-argument that our organization is a victim of frequent labour management problem. Strikes and lockouts are common but in recent days it is quite different because of several changes in the policy level. The labour management relationship is not as appreciable in the maintenance of industrial harmony and climate. Let me tell, here in our organization, from time immemorial the trade unions have powerful influence upon decision-making of organisation. Majority of the unions in our organization have strong affiliation with political organizations. The culture of Kerala also has the culture of "Atti mari" workers and the state is famous for their trade union militancy. The policy of 'militancy' is indirectly supported even by the government. Majority of the existing employees in the organizations have membership in any of the trade unions. The strong support from trade unions is to fight for their rights. Since management has created a culture of mistrust and suspicion among the organizational members, it is difficult for the trade unions to convince members, to organize themselves for the sake of organization. The threat of downsizing and divestment compelled the trade unions to fight for the rights and privileges of members of the organisation, since there is a probability to losing many of their privileges in the near future. So the cooperation of the two groups are at mirage.

When I joined in this organization, I didn't have a political affiliation or backup with any of the trade unions. The relation between management and workers was strained as it was. Though I belong to a management cadre now, I know situations, where the management has victimized employees without giving proper attention and justification to the act done. Employee's tendency to join trade unions started as and when they perceive the relationship between themselves and management strained and subjective in implementation of grievances and the redressal procedures initiated by the management.

Let me tell frankly, till now I don't have any conflicting interaction with any of the workers or managerial officer, in the organisation. One may ask why, because, I don't have that much courage to fight with any one of them considering the long-term relationship and impact. I would not have reached this position if I had engaged myself in any of the organisational or individual conflict. Many times situations compelled me to fight with the management. As I said above, because of my selfish interests, I reserved commends of mine, that I just didn't want to make any rift with the management. The organization has history of several such cases, where few lost their career because of this rift with management. There are many such stories, where management had taken corporal steps as punitive measure.

The attitude of supervisory members was bossy type and is autocratic in style of leadership and management. They simply have to follow the decisions taken by the management rather than formulation of any policies. They never participate with workers in decision-making processes. In majority of departments supervisors or the top level management takes decisions and they use workers only at implementation level. The supervisors are status oriented. They never mingled so closely with workers either in work environment or outside. Actually, for the sake of existence, managers are compelled to follow the code of conduct. If any one of them goes against the cord of conduct, he or she will become the scapegoat of the situation. Since I belonged to a part of management at present, I too was following the code for the sake of existence and to avoid the wrath of management.

Since majority of activities are top-down in nature, the environment could not develop any teamwork within organization. It is true that some of the departments have a good teamwork where superiors are providing supportive climate for group work. The superiors take important decisions on group emphasis rather than centralized decision-making process. Beyond the superiors instruction there is no group at all. But generally such attitude cannot be found in majority of departments.

Now I can tell you that the culture of the organization do not promote a participative job environment where innovative initiation and risk taking are promoted. Basically, the management does not want to communicate any prime decisions to low level members. They don't have any practice of sharing information, which are detrimental to the organizational existence. Lack of sharing of information has developed antagonistic attitude within the employees and the union. It further enhances lack of trust and confidence among members towards management.

In the initial days, such things caused severe problems between trade unions and managements. Now a days, because of political back up of trade unions, the culture of sharing information at least for certain extent is recognized by the management. The autocratic style of management preferred by top authorities is still reluctant to communicate major decisions with employees since it would create headache to organizational management. I feel that majority of public sector industrial organizations are maintaining the culture of administration. Even though I belong to management, I couldn't justify some of the militant decisions taken by the management. Still I am confused to know who are militant in its approach.

I identified major problems in the organizations as grievance procedure handling, a free and fair reward system, rules and regulations, communication, trade unions, political back up, and the like. The wage given by the management to the workers found to be quite reasonable when compared to several other organizations nearby. I don't know whether my opinion is same as that of other members in this organization. But I am satisfied with my package. My family is solely depending on my salary for their daily sustenance. And it is true that, with one income, it is difficult for a four-membered family to survive. I also had to face severe financial problems in my life. But this doesn't mean that the salary I am receiving is quite bad. Believe me I am not justifying the management. The workers are also getting fair amount of wage. But, the reward system, related to incentives and bonuses are inviting disagreement and conflicts between labourers and the management. Mainly on bonus issues, organizations had to face several strikes. Here, I will blame workers that even in the severe financial loss, and organizational turmoil company flowed reasonable bonus every year. Without understanding the financial crises of the company trade union led which agitations are not found good for existence of companies' in future. The workers are not ready to understand or support the management of company because this company management recently supported the disinvestments policies of central government.

As far as incentive system is concerned, management does not have any practice of appreciating the worker performance and recognizing their effort. As far as promotion policy is concerned even in the public sector many manipulations are a regular feature. It has the belief that seniority will be the criteria for promotion in public sector industrial establishment. But in majority cases the top level management decision influence in the selection of names for promotion. The promotions are not frequent and members have to wait for long years to fulfill majority criteria stipulated for promotion. Moreover, if the individual members are in the black list of management, their promotion will be deliberately delayed by pointing some of the inefficiencies to disqualify. Though I have 25 years of experience in this organization I have obtained only limited number of promotional opportunities in my occupational life. This doesn't mean that I have created any problem to the management but this is the usual procedure in every public sector industrial establishment. There is more stagnation in this sector. I feel that in private sector industrial establishments, this is not the situation. There, more than seniority the merit of employee will be taken into consideration for promotion. Those who work hard have plenty of opportunities for career advancement and enrichment. And there are limited criteria for disqualifying the candidate's opportunities for selection. Even every member in the organization is informed about the promotional policies and criteria for selection. Here in public sector there is no clear-cut understanding about the promotional policies of management and the government.

Another aspect I would like to share is that the technological culture of the organization. The organization is very poor in maintaining the present technology and reluctant to introduce new machineries. The technological culture of the organization doesn't promote any new skill or knowledge in the operation of production process. Moreover the life of the worker with in organizational setting is hazardous in nature, since the production processes are with outdated machineries. Though there are plenty of welfare measure ensured for employee's health and safety, these policies are inadequate to consider the value of life.

Since the management is facing sever financial constraints it cannot think about rationalization in organization. But introduction of new technology will any way bring profit and production and better quality of life to the organization. Instead of introducing new machineries, now a days management is engaged in reduction of labour force and other by manpower planning strategies to curb the financial constrains. Which means that management is not labour supportive or proactive. The attitude towards downsizing has created severe opposition from workers and trade unions. But the contrary situation is that many people are opting voluntary retirement scheme proposed by the management. Never in the history of organization, we heard of a situation where management had taken such a serious decision to downsize the work force, to curb the financial turbulence in the management. It has created mistrust and suspicion among employees on management intention towards employment. It has developed anxiety and depression among employees. Many opted VRS, and the reason for opting voluntary retirement scheme is on personal ground rather than any other professional reasons.

Many senior employers and employees are found to opt the voluntary retirement scheme because of many reasons viz., repayment of schemes, marriage of their daughters, and other personal reasons. Many experienced employees opted VRS since they got better employment due to their expertise in specific field. Another reason is that, if there any initiation of privatization, their employment is at stake. They are all uncertain of the consequences of disinvestments policy and further management approach. Employees believe that the rigid rules and regulations and other organizational factors will further be tightened in order to control the behaviour of employees rather putting effort to understand the problems of employees. To avoid these uncertainties in future majority senior employees and employers have opted for voluntary retirement scheme. I believe that majority of the employees won't accept voluntary retirement scheme because majority of the families depends solely on their wages for daily sustenance. I am not at all interested to opt voluntary retirement scheme, since it would create severe financial problems in my family. I believe that the culture of downsizing will not produce any concrete results in long term. The consequences of downsizing policies will result in loss of, many experienced and talented employees from organization. Management has to appoint skilled laborers in order to tackle the situation that is caused by severe labour turnover. It is not necessary that the new skilled labour would be able to cope up with the outdated technology and the technical knowledge. Those skills will not have any significance since changes and modification in the technology is required. Employees feel uncertain bout their future life in the organization till their retirement. This means that it would affect the quality of life of the retainers. Somebody term it as 'Retainer's Syndrome.'

The induction programs included under socialization process are not be updated and will not produce any new values and ethical behaviour. It will not help an employee to internalize the norms and values of organization. It will not help them in developing additional organizational interest or facilitate development of personality. The socialization programs are only for namesake. It is inculcating only limited knowledge in the specialized area of functional importance to the newcomers. The training programs of management and that of workers varied considerably. The employers have to get training in labour management strategies rather than developing any other programs. How to manage conflict is of priority for management training. From the very beginning of training programs the basic objective of management is to indoctrinate the young management professionals, how to pamper the trade unions and employee tactfully in order to maintain the statuesque of management domination over employees. The processes of socialization frankly speaking, do not have any importance at all. A new employee learns the organizational practices more from other agents of socialization, which include the peer groups, co-workers etc, rather than from any of the managerial person. Since centralized-approach is going on, no one dares to ask any clarification in the procedural irregularities of the organization. Moreover in a culture of strange labour management relation, there wont have any useful knowledge that is to be passed on to new employees.

Majority cultural traits are mixed with mistrust, in an autocratic values system. The organization does not have any good experience and practice that can be shared with new employees and take the pride of organizational identity. The orientation programs cannot induce new values, which facilitate new members to have better adjustment with the job and organization. Here the role of trade union should not be neglected just the management they are also socializing employees to develop hostile attitude towards practices of management. They have plenty of stories, strange incidents and actions taken by the management against laborers, pointing out severe marginalization and atrocities. I have an opinion that both management and trade union are equally influenced by the value system and sow the seeds of antagonistic attitude within employees and employers.

The Hope

I don't believe that where there is strange relationship between management and workers is there any chance for good socialization process and programs. And, further I believe that effective socialization programs lies where there is opportunities for sharing deep rooted values and good experiences that an organization consider as mile stones. Moreover where there is mutual trust and cooperation between employees and employers and where there is creation of better impression about the practice of organization there is a chance for sharing of information related to the culture of organization that need to be followed by the members of the organisation. Where there rigid rules and regulations control over behaviors of members and autocratic styles of leadership, the employees have to share only the atrocities against them and the irregularities followed to curb employee's behaviour that in tune with the system. In this context, I would like to commend that, as I said earlier, trade unions and the management has key role in establishing a new culture of high performance. Here the slogan of socialization process should to familiarize the organizational values and beliefs with employees, rather than to fight against one. The socialization process should insure effective coping up of life with job environment. The training programs should facilitate and should up date in order to induce strong cultural values to the organizational members to develop trust and confidence.

The strained labour management relationship has developed antagonistic attitude among employees and employers. The employees have strong disagreement with the welfare policies of the organization in certain areas. Though the company is providing transport facilities, educational assistance and other programs they are very slow in providing medical facilities and reimbursements. The management has the version that welfare provision itself is a financial burden on the company. The company exists not for making any profit but also for providing welfare facilities to the employers and to the employees. The innumerable welfare schemes are introduced by the government is actually misused by the employees and has made them more lazy if they work only money. I believe that management is providing innumerable welfare facilities to the members and there are welfare provisions. To a great extent the culture of welfare might have created a hedonistic and assertive culture among workers. People are more concentrated on welfare rights rather than the duties and service.

If one asks me about my feelings towards job satisfaction, in fact, I have only mixed impression on it. The atmosphere of the organization is not is not suitable enough to develop job satisfaction. Yes, reward, in general motivate employees, but I believe that more than rewards, the facilities and welfare may be the motivating factors for employee's. The strained relationship between the members and management is another factor, which develop dissatisfaction. There is no and democratic style of management to serve and support employees.

Let me add few more on the definition I have already stated on Culture. To me the culture of an organization is the deep-rooted belief of the organizational members. A believe that everyone supports each other and understands each other well. There won't be any miscommunication between the management and laborers. There should be collective consciousness rather than individual, self motivated interest and identity. I have the belief that a strong cultural practices develop, strong committed feeling with in individuals towards the organization and to abide by the rules and regulations of the organization and the preferred patterns of behaviors widely accepted and held at large. Instead of having hard feeling towards rules and regulations management should communicate, the very purpose of norms and control.

I have strong belief that teamwork is not suitable for all organizational set up. Where it is suitable, there is need to be implemented. But, here in this organisation, integration between different departments should be encouraged to work. A functional flexibility is to be provided to the organizational members for making an at effective decisions. A good technical knowledge would facilitate smooth progress of work without making any wastage in production process and will improve the quality of products. To improve the efficiency of workers effective material and non-material incentive system should be implemented which is now alien to present culture. Proper recognition of employees on target accomplishment should be encouraged and there should be appropriate incentive system. The reward criteria should also be taken into account for the fair promotion policies incorporating both seniority and merit.

Training and developmental programs should incorporate other career development and personality development programs. Emphasis should be given to health and safety of employers. Policies against workers interest should not be taken and militant policies like downsizing, etc should not be considered. Since it would develop antagonistic attitude, because of fear and anxiety about uncertainty, such decisions should be arrived only when the system ensures mutual discussion between employees and employers. The grievance handling procedure will be effective only when it develops accountability to the procedure adopted by the management. The trust and confidence of dispute machineries should be developed.

A system of high-performance culture must concentrate on human resources of the organization and its effective utilization.

Let me conclude this self-interaction. I would like to end up this self-interaction by making a comment that the *culture is "the way we do things around here". It is the shared beliefs, values, norms and traditions within the organization.*

Questions

1. Relate the reality and hope. Discuss the hard realties for a better hope.
2. What are the underlying ethos members in the organisation widely held?
3. Differentiate a weak work culture and strong work culture?
4. Do you believe that a reality check will help organisation to develop a strong work culture?
5. Develop a strategy that helps in the creation of strong culture?
6. Relate the work culture concept of in relation to soft and synergetic work culture?

Case 22

ORGANISATIONAL CULTURE AND MOTIVATION

Sidan Steel and Power Ltd (SSPL) is a part of US$ 12 billion Sidan Organisation after consolidating their positions as a leading player in steel, power, mining, oil and gas, and infrastructure sectors in India. They have expanded their business to other parts of the world, particularly in Asia, (Indonesia, Nepal, Mangolia), Africa, South America, and Gerogia. In India, the company has its flagship steel plant at Chattisgarh and Jamshedpur.

The company promotes a family culture and literally takes care of both employees and their family members through various programs and measures. The company extends all the statutory and non statutory measures for the health, welfare and safety of employees. Since the employees has to move from one location to another for operational purpose their children's education, housing facilities, transportation, etc all are looked after well by the company. Further company believes that the employee's family support to them is very crucial in undertaking their roles and responsibilities effectively. Employees who genuinely approached the company with a real need were given all the help that was necessary.

Mr. Vinod Pandey started his career in Sidan Steel and Power Ltd (SSPL) as Company Secretary at a fairly senior level from 1998 onwards. He worked at abroad and handled additional responsibilities of corporate affairs for 9 years. The company called him back to India in their Chhattisgarh Office, as Manager Corporate Affairs in a period of 15 days. When he had to relocate himself from abroad to Chhattisgarh the company went all out to ensure that everything was taken care of. The department provided all the domestic facilities such as a new house which is well furnished, and schooling for his kids and logistic support so that all his personal effects could be moved. He could settle in his new position, roles and responsibilities in a period of 15 days. He was so happy in his new roles and the facilities and the support extended to his family members.

However, his enthusiasm was short-lived, when a disaster struck the family; his daughter was diagnosed to be suffering from cancer. She has started her schooling in the new school very shortly. To get admission in that prestigious school the company had made very good effort. The incident was very painful to Mr. Vinod Pandey and his family members. Before engaging himself with the new roles and responsibilities he was stuck to this family issue. The doctors advised him to start with more diagnosis in any of the specialized hospitals in cities, for best treatment if possible. Mr. Vinod Pandey was so perplexed in the juncture since his daughter required immediate attention and thinking about his new assignments and house holds.

The HR department of Sidan Steel and Power Ltd (SSPL) came to know about this issue from the employees. They verified all the employment record of Mr. Vinod Pandey for the past 10 years. They came to know that Mr. Vinod Pandey is one among the best managerial staff in the company and proved his merit in discharging his functional responsibilities abroad. The Vice President of HR called Mr. Vinod Pandey to his chamber and intimated the company decision to him. He informed that Mr. Vinod Pandey doesn't have to attend office on regular basis as he had to take his daughter for treatment. The company is ready to bear the huge costs for drugs, radiation as well as chemo-therapy and alternate arrangements for young children to be coached. The facilities department would provide for the personal care and assistance of everything viz. payment of bills, escorting Mr. Vinod Pandey's daughter for treatment, selection of the right doctors, support for his daughters continuous education and like all other necessary requirements.

The Vice President HR informed through a formal letter to Mr. Vinod Pandey that "Since you have been taking care of the very interests of the organisation for the pat 10 years and working towards its integrity and growth, it's our moral responsibility to take care of you and your family in return.... We would be extending all our facilities and service to you and your family so that we bring happiness and prosperity back in your life."

The company stood by its words that they had been given to Mr. Vinod Pandey. Utmost care has been given to his daughter in getting better treatment from one of the best hospitals in city. After 6 months of rigorous treatment his daughter recovered from the ailment. When his family has returned back to company quarters, the company arranged a warm welcome. The Vice President himself was present in the function.

Questions

1. How HR practices become role model in this case?
2. Evaluate the message from the case.
3. How does the company evaluate employee significance?
4. How do you judge the moral responsibilities of a business organisation in relation to personal crisis situation?
5. Discuss the organisational culture that motivates employees to be with organisation.

CASE 23

ORGANIZATIONAL POLITICS AND STRIKE

XYZ, Delhi, has around 18000 employees. It has excellent employee participation formal welfare amenities including a 100 bed hospital with the treatment of ultra modern facilities.

The shop floors of the factory, biggest of its kind in India, have huge heavy duty over load cranes handle turbans and other heavy equipments and components.

On a particular day twenty year old Christian boy, Mr. Biju employed on temporary basis, fell down from a height of 50 feet, while working on a crane. He sustain severe head injury and was rushed to XYZ hospital. Because of his bad luck, he died within few hours inspite of the best medical attention.

Since the mother of the diseased worker was away in Kerala,, his father, who himself is a regular employee of XYZ, requested the hospital authorities o preserve the dead body in the hospital mortuary. On the third day after the mother arrived, the father with some of his close relatives went to collect the dead body. The father and others were shocked to see the body in a decomposed state. Then only it was realized that the refrigerating unit of mortuary was not working properly. The father refused to take delivery of the body.

The news spread like wildfire. The hundred of workers and relatives present there were very much agitated over its unfortunate happening. The union leaders were informed. They demanded the immediate dismissal of the doctors who were in charge of the ICU on the day of the accident and also other doctors connected with the incident.

The Chief Executive and GM personnel visited the hospital immediately. Annoyed by the occurring and the agonizing sight they ordered immediate suspension of the then doctor in charge of the ICU. However, the agitated workers and the trade union leaders were not satisfied.

The Union is demanding dismissal of doctor or else they would continue the strike. Father is un relenting and is still refusing to accept the body.

Meanwhile,. Doctors and the colleagues through IMA, Delhi, branch met the GM Personnel and demanded immediate withdrawal of suspension of the doctor. If not, they would go on the strike immediately. They maintained that it is not the duty of the doctor to look after refrigeration unit of the mortuary.

Discussion Question

1. Discuss organisational politics and pressure tactics in tune with the case study.
2. How you relate the case with Factory Act. With reference to factory act discuss the case in detail.
3. Discuss the stand of GM personnel and the trade union leaders.

CASE 24

PROFESSIONAL ETHICS

Sai Nath Institute of Science and Technology, is one of the famous Institute located at Kottayam, Kerala. This institute has one engineering college, Applied Science Institute and a few undergraduate courses. The Engineering College got its best academic training status within a period of 5years. The placement of the Engineering College was fine and many companies like Infosys, Wipro, Cognizent, Eisher, Tata, Samsung, LG Electronics, Whirlpool etc already selected students from the campus. The better placement scenario and the academic reputation had compelled the institute management to start an MBA programme from July Academic Year onwards. They have got the permission to run an MBA programme from Mahatma Gandhi University, Kottayam.

Though many advertisements have been floated in major dailies, they didn't get proper response from the good faculty members in business management subjects. The institute has faced difficulty in getting better faculty members from within and outside the state. Since the location of the institute was interior to Kottayam many faculty members who applied for the vacancies and selected and they further have dropped their plan to join the organisation. The institute do not have any permanent building to show and convince the faculty whom they have selected, with modern facilities that to attract and retain them. More over the institute has not offered better pay packages and accommodation facilities to the faculty members who were ready to join. The structure of the management institute has a guesthouse-converted building with a single classroom, office room and conference room. But they have communicated to the interested faculty members that they would allot a new building for the institute within the campus, within a period of 3 and half month. The location of the institute was to face many difficulties like the transportation and communication facilities. No STD booths near by to college and there were limited number of line bus through the institute rout. The students of engineering colleges and applied sciences were staying at Hostel.

Ms. Kavitha Shanmugham, M.Phill, PhD has joined as Faculty in Human Resource Management in Sai Nath Institute of Management, at Kottayam, Kerala. She has been working as faculty of HR in one of the premier business management school in Chennai. Within a period of four years she has developed her reputation as a soft skill trainer. Her background in Psychology had given her better opportunity to known as a mentor and counselor to the business graduate students and as a practitioner in the implementation of Psychometric tests. Her skills and expertise had been utilized by her previous institute in the student's selection and training process. Every time she got better appreciation from the Director and faculties of previous institute on her academic contributions commitment and hard work. Her decision to switch over from Chennai to Kerala was based on family concern. The family pressure compelled her to join in any of the institute in Kerala. When she returned majority institute has already closed their selection process for the faculties. Quiet fortunately, she had seen the advertisement of Sai Nath Institute of Management, Kottayam. Immediately she applied for the post of faculty/trainer Sai Nath Institute of Management. She got the offer letter stating that the institute would be providing single accommodation facility and free mess to the faculty. Believing the offer letter and the appointment order from the Sai Nath Institute of Management, she has joined the institute in the stipulated date.

She took all her belongings from Chennai to the institute. She has been allotted a single room within the hostel. When she entered the room, she has got annoyed by seeing another three beds inside the room. The room didn't have a table and a chair to study. She enquired the matter with the Dean Welfare. The Dean welfare replied that he didn't have any intimation from the institute management to give her a single room with a table and a chair. She stayed within the hostel during that night with two girl students of Applied Sciences. On the next day morning she took up the matter to the Dean SIM (Sai Nath Institute of Management). By giving hope to her he assured Kavitha that the issue will be settled within few days. Mean while the Director of the institute landed for a discussion with the Dean. She raised the issue to him and the Director also assured her that within two - three days the issue would be settled. She agreed to the Director's assurance and adjusted herself with the limited facilities offered to her. Mean while her accommodaton has been transferred from one hostel to another. She had to take her entire belonging from one hostel to the another.

She started her preparation to the Course launch programme on the coming Monday. The Dean has given her the responsibility of compeering of all programmes, since she found that she was in good in communication and presentation skills. She agreed the responsibility. On Friday, she asked the Dean about her accommodation. The Dean assured her that he would call the CEO and arrange her accommodation that day itself. But she informed the Dean that she wouldn't be attending the launch programme, if they couldn't be able to arrange her accommodation that day before evening. She informed him further that as per the direction and assurance she waited the arrangement till date. But there was no communication from either the Dean or the CEO or the Director. The Dean called CEO immediately and asked him about the arrangement made for the accommodation of the lady faculty. The Director called the CEO enquired about the same. As such there was no paper arrangement, the Director asked the Dean (SIM) to wait another couple of days for the arrangement. The Dean informed the same to Kavita. She got very much annoyed by listening to the Dean's reply. Without giving any second thought in the matter she informed the Dean that she would be leaving that evening to her home taking all of her luggage and not attending the launch programme on Monday. She further asked the Dean to inform whether the arrangement would be made for her in the hostel or not. Till then she would be staying at her home.

The Dean once again called the CEO and the Director and reported the matter. The institute has four faculty members at present to run the entire programmed. He informed the Director and CEO of the institute that loosing one faculty was not advisable before the launch programme. It would affect the image of the institute before the parent and students, who are the major stakeholders. He informed the Director that with limited infrastructure and inadequate number of faculty members we couldn't run the business school. The matter became so hot in the corporate office. The CEO called the Dean Welfare and asked the availability of the accommodation. By obtaining a negative reply, the CEO further tried to get an accommodation in the YWCA. They got accommodation in the YWCA. The arrangement were then made and was communicated to Kavitha. She then raised the offer of free food. During night the institute would not be able to arrange food to her. More over she has to travel 15 Kilometers from the City to the institute every day. She then asked about the travel facility. The institute offered her the engineering college student bus. Now she asked everything in writing. But the institute was not ready to give her in writing. The Director informed her that they can extend the facility only to that extends and the better accommodation will be provided after three months.

Once again problem popped up. She requested the Dean not make further proceeding in this matter. Within five minutes she forwarded her resignation letter to the Dean. The Dean became so annoyed by seeing her resignation letter. He called the CEO and the Director and informed the development. The administration couldn't reach a solution till evening. In the evening hours the CEO called the Dean of Students Welfare and ordered him to arrange the accommodation within the hostel with a separate bathroom for faculties and free mess at that hostel.

By getting another arrangement offer from the administration Kavitha became so annoyed. The decision on accommodation has subjected to change every time. She thought, if this would be the style of making decision of management, she would be facing more difficult situation from the institute. By hearing the new arrangement offer Kavitha became so happy. Her offer at last got materialized.

But she made a second thought on whether to accept it or not. She made a self-analysis on the issue.

- The management didn't understand the concern and anxieties of a lady faculty with regard to the lack of accommodation.
- The management didn't follow their promises and offer given. They violated their promises by allocating her accommodation to a 3-bed, single room in the hostel without basic facilities.
- The management changed her accommodation from one hostel to another within a period of three days.
- The management tried to arrange the accommodation in YWCA, which is far away from the institution in the city.
- The management was not ready to give free mess facility when they arranged accommodation outside the institute.
- The management changed their decision by not giving promised accommodation within a period of 3 months.
- Within a period of three to four days the management changed their decisions many times ignoring all the promises given to a faculty.

After this self-analysis she became so silent. Her conscience was continuously advising her not to join in an organization where the leaders didn't follow their word. She called her father asked a second opinion. Her father asked her that 'if an organization couldn't plan, organize and manage even the basic facilities to those who ready to serve the organization, how they could be able to teach management to their students. He suggested her to resign. By getting the reply from her father she asked the Dean to follow the resignation letter that she had already given to the Director.

She wrote a simple letter to the Director of the institute before she left the campus and handed over the same to the Dean.

The letter can be illustrated as follows

From

Kavitha Shanmugham
Faculty
Sai Institute of Management
Kottayam

To

The Director
Sai Nath Institute of Management
Kottayam

Respected Sir,

Hope this letter finds with you in the best of health and spirits.

As you are aware I have been knocking your door since my joining in this organisation regarding my accommodation. I have observed lot of changes in the promises that you have given me in this regard. At last you arranged an accommodation where I settled first. Mean while many times you have changed my accommodation from one hostel to another. I found there is a great discrepancy between what you offered and what you have given. I don't work for an organization that does not follow its promises and words. I believe that the greatest asset in human life is keeping the promises that one has given to somebody. As a leader of the organization if you couldn't follow your word by keeping the ethical practices in the front line, better not to teach the students the ethics and professional ethics in doing business. It could only help you to produce unscrupulous and unethical professional beings to run the business rather that ethical business graduates.

Let me share all of my concern with you at least in the last day of my job in this institution. It's my humble request to you that kindly don't give promises to people if you cannot follow it. Kindly consider this letter as "letter of resignation" from my part.

Expecting your professional ethics in your future endeavors,

Thanking you,

Yours Sincerely,

(Kavitha Shanmugham)

Discussion Questions

1. Do you believe that professional ethics is an important factor in management of an organization?
2. Quality and output lies on ethical decision-making. How you perceive this comment.
3. Major managerial approaches can be perceived through value driven activities. Discuss.
4. Analyze the managerial style of the institute leaders in relation to various incidents.
5. To what extent ethics is important in professional interaction and inter relationship at work. Discuss.
6. Differentiate preaching and practice?

Case 25

PEOPLE AND ORGANIZATIONAL STRUCTURE

Prof. Kiran has been working as a Faculty in Human Resource Management, in one of the prestigious Business Management institutes in Pune. Though he employed at Pune, he has been registered for PhD in one the universities, near by his native place, in Kerala. He has finished his Doctoral thesis in Organizational Behaviour, in the month of April 2005 and decided to submit the thesis for adjudication and evaluation in the month of May 2005. The institute has extended 10 days leave to Kiran for the submission of PhD thesis, even in the midst of responsibilities on admission of new batch of students, conduction of entrance test, interviews and selection during May/June months.

On 1st May, the Labour Day, he reached Kerala. As per the intimation from his friends he had prepared all the documents for the submission of PhD thesis. On May 2nd he reached at the University for the thesis submission objective. Though the guide has given some idea to Kiran, regarding the submission procedures, he decided to clarify the same with the information counter. Since the campus spread over with many blocks and buildings and he didn't know the department from where he would get information about the submission procedures, Kiran waited in front of the information counter to collect the details. He waited there till 10.45am to see some staff in the information counter and clarify with appropriate information. Meanwhile he had better interaction with the peons of the centre and he came to know the procedural delays and regular lazy routine of the university employees towards their duties and responsibilities.

The university bus came only at 10.45am. He saw many staff members running towards their concerned departments. The staffs of information counter were present in their seat only at 11.00am. The peons of the centre have been waiting there to get their signature and send the attendance register to the administrative block. The information counter was already filled up with huge crowed. The telephone of the information counter was ringing from early morning. But no staff, including the peons, showed their interest to attend the phone calls. As soon as the staff seated on their chairs they ordered 'Tea' to the peon. The peons went to get the Tea for the 'officers'. The staff started talking with each other ignoring the huge crowed in front of the centre. Loosing the patience some of the parents started asking information from the staff. When one parent argued with the officer, the staff replied with arrogance that 'go and lodge a complaint against us to the Vice Chancellor.' The officers gave better message to the information seekers that 'this is the routine of the university procedures and they all have to wait for the officer's mercy'.

The work started at 11.30am, only after getting 'Tea' to the officers. After 10-12 information seekers Kiran got the opportunity to ask clarification on PhD submission. The information officer without looking at Kiran's face replied that 'go to AC-X department and get all clarifications from there'. Understanding the nature of the officer, Kiran, once again humbly asked, 'Sir, which building?' The officer replied without having a helping tone that 'go left and turn right'. He started to attend the person next to Kiran. Since the campus is filled up with so many buildings Kiran has to face difficulty in the identification of AC-X building. After searching for 15-20 minutes in the campus, he found AC-X department, which was located in the Controller of Examination Building.

The lady staff of the AC-X department detailed all information related to submission of PhD to Kiran. She asked him to submit the adjudication form with 11 synopses and the forwarding letter from the Director of the school of studies. Understanding the multifarious task associated with the submission procedure, he came out of the department searching for the adjudication form. One of the staff members directed him to the general store of the university from where all forms were available. When he reached there, the staff asked him to show the cash bill. Since he didn't know the procedure, the staff simply replied that 'go to cash counter and get the slip from there. After a long search on the second floor of the 7th building where the State Bank of India's office situated, he saw a small cash center with a huge crowed in front. Having a centralized counter, payment to all forms and other purposes to be made there. He waited there in the queue till his turn came. Collecting the slip from the cash counter he rushed to the general store. When he reached there the store closed for noon session. One of the staff advised him to come at 2.00pm to collect the form. Kiran, without even having lunch, waited near by the store till the opening time. The office resumed its functions, but only at 2.30pm, after the lunch session. Majority of the staff were found sleepy. He collected the form and without wasting time, rushed to School of Studies to meet his guide for further proceedings.

The School of Studies has only limited staff. The department consists of four faculties and three administrative staff including one peon. It is known to every one that to get things done from the department the wards have to depend on 'peons' than the 'Director.' With lump sum amount of money everything can be done within minutes and seconds. But Kiran couldn't meet his guide, since he has taken three days leave for attending one workshop. Kiran become frustrated and worried, since he had only ten-days leave for the thesis submission purpose.

After 3 days on May 5th, he got signature and further assistance from the guide and he directed Kiran to get the approval from the Director. The conflict between the Director and Kiran's guide has been widely known to department, after having their struggle to get into the position of Directorship. After taking the adjudication form, the Director asked him to clear all the dues from various departments and submit the same day. She asked Kiran to produce all the due certificates, from general library, department library and other departments at the earliest. Kiran neither used department library nor the university library, for his research purpose. Still the Director asked him to produce certificate from there. In search of library Kiran started another trip. Finally he found the university library. When he reached there the librarian was on leave for three days. The librarian had taken the leave without giving charge to any one. Kiran felt, that things are causing much trouble. With an empty hand he returned to the department. While on the way he met the departmental peon Mr. Joseph. Kiran described the entire problem to Joseph. Kiran asked his help by offering better 'return.' Joseph took up the assignment. Taking all the details Joseph went on to get the dues certificate. Two hours later he came back with the all dues certificates. Kiran got so surprised to see it. Having all the dues certificates when he reached the Director's cabin he was informed that the Director has already left the campus. Joseph informed him that the Director would be on leave for the next day also.

On 7th May, Kiran produced all the dues certificates with other documents to the Director. She signed all the documents and returned back with 'best of luck.' With the adjudication form, 11 synopses, the panel list of the evaluators and the forwarding letters once again he reached AC X department with Joseph. While looking upon the document the lady staff informed him that he has not paid the adjudication fee. An amount of Rs.2500/- required to be paid as adjudication fee. Once again Kiran reached the cash counter and has collected the Chelan slip of 2500/Rs. Kiran requested the help of Joseph in the further proceedings, since he has been facing many hurdles from the departments. Joseph agreed to help him. Joseph took the entire documents and submitted the same to the lady staff. Since, Joseph has better relationship with the departmental staff, he succeeded in submission of synopsis within few minutes. On May 7 th submission of PhD synopsis got over.

Joseph informed him that he has to wait for another three months for the submission of the thesis as per the university norms. Now the synopsis-forwarding step has completed. Joseph told him that the submission of the thesis depends on 'how you make the follow up' with various departments in the coming days.... if you make effective follow up, you can submit your thesis within one moth. The clearance file required to be verified by many officials at various hierarchical levels. The clearance file has to move from AC X department to PhD section, from there to Assistant Registrar, from Assistant Registrar to Deputy Registrar, from Deputy Registrar to Joint Registrar, from Joint Registrar to Registrar the same file should return in the same manner to the PhD section and from there to the AC X department. By hearing all these university hierarchical hurdles, for the PhD submission, Kiran became so tensed and frustrated. He thought the only way to reduce the days in these hierarchical hurdles is to pay a lump sum amount to Joseph and get it done at the earliest. Kiran offered better 'return' to the peon and requested his help by explaining his problem related to job. The peon agreed to do it. He asked Kiran to come after three days since the Registrar and other officials were engaged in personal interviews on permanent posts at various levels in the university. Having no option he returned home with tension and anxiety.

It's almost one week over. Meanwhile many calls from the institute came for his requirement in the recruitment and selection process for the new batch. He sent a letter to the Director seeking one week more leave from the institute. The institute rejected the request and asked him to come back within 2-3 days. The Director had given the option either to leave the job or come back within 2-3 days. Kiran's tension and frustration became so high by hearing the reply from the institute Director. If he continued here with university procedures it would end up with lose of job. But he thought, without PhD Degree he has only limited career options. Any way, once he has to go through all these university dealings for the submission of thesis, either today or tomorrow. He decided to continue his effort for the submission of PhD and sent another letter, requesting one week leave from the institute.

On 10th May as per the direction of the peon he reached the university department. In the university, Joseph has got the clearance from the Deputy Registrar of the AC X department and forwarded the file to the Controller of Examination for his close scrutiny. While, Joseph came to know that the Controller of Examination of examination was on official trip to some of the regional centres of the university for monitoring and evaluation. Joseph informed Kiran that the Controller of Examination would be coming only May 13th. On May 13th as usual Kiran and Joseph approached the Controller of Examination office. The file was not signed. The peon picked up the file and sought help from one of the attenders of the Examination Department to place the file on the top of all files. After one hour Joseph got the signed file and started their journey to PhD section.

The Ph.D Section is very famous for creating obstacle to the research scholars. There is no proper documentation system. Conflict between the research scholars and the department staffs is quite common. The Administrative Assistant of the PhD section is an egocentric person, showing his power and authority, more than the Section Officer. Being the leader of one of the strong university employees unions, gives more importance to the to union activities than the day-to-day departmental responsibilities. One couldn't see him more than one hour in his seat in a day. But no one dared to complaint against him, since he has strong hold on employees union and create unnecessary hurdles to the research scholars. His past history detailed many stories of missing files, progress reports and original papers. Though the file reached on 13th May, to the Ph D session, it was blocked there till 17th of May because of Administrative Assistant's absence on his seat. On 17th of May Administrative Assistant wrote a note and passed the file to the verification of the Section officer. The Section officer's signed the clearance file as soon as it reached there. Joseph took the file to the next hierarchical level for verification, the Assistant Registrar.

When the file reached the Assistant Registrar, Joseph couldn't see her. She has been attending a meeting at Deputy Registrar Level since morning. The peon kept the clearance file on the top of all the files. Joseph asked Kiran to wait there till the file gets signed. The file once again got blocked there for one day. On 19th May, the Assistant Registrar passed the clearance file to the Deputy Registrar. When the file reached up to the Deputy Registrar cabin, one union meeting was going on. The leaders of the union of Deputy Registrars were discussing on an upcoming employee strike. The desk in front of Deputy Registrar was filled up with many files. Since the peon belongs to the Deputy Registrar's union they allowed him to enter into the cabin. Without looking up to the files Deputy Registrar signed the clearance files. The clearance file moved from Deputy Registrar to the Joined Registrar. The Joined Registrar cabin was found empty as other departments. The departmental peon informed Joseph about an urgent meeting at Registrar level where the Joint Registrars had to attend. He told further that the meeting would continue till evening. Cursing the system of the University Kiran returned home.

He called one of his friends and asked about the developments in the institute. But he couldn't give any information on institutional affairs.

On 20th May the Joint Registrar signed the clearance file and passed on the same to Registrar. Kiran got the information that the Registrar is been attending an important meeting at Vice Chancellors room in relation to upcoming Syndicate Meeting. He is not ready to look any files on the coming two days because of the urgency of syndicate meeting. Now these dialogues became so casual to Kiran and he didn't respond to it. On 22 nd the Registrar signed the paper and gave back the same to the Assistant Registrar. When the files reached up to Assistant Registrar it was around 4.00pm. The Assistant Registrar already left her office and the peon asked them to come on next day. On 23 rd May the Assistant Registrar signed the file and passed the file to the PhD section. The Section officer put the file of the Administrative Assistant and asked Kiran to wait for a while. The Administrative Assistant came at 3.30pm. The peon personally requested the Administrative Assistant to speed up the file. He took the file and started writing. Till 4.30pm he continued the writing. With a note he passed on the file further to the AC X department. The peon took the file and run towards AC X department. As and when they reached there the staffs were already get into University bus. Since it was weekend, there was less hope for the submission of thesis for next two days. The concerned lady in the department asked him to come on 25 th.

On 25th May, the Deputy Registrar of the AC X department allowed the submission of thesis to the Examination Department. Kiran submitted four copies of the thesis to the university and gave big thanks to the university authorities. A three months target for thesis submission thus finished within a period of 25 days. He understood the 'value of Joseph's (Peons)' help in getting things done in a university. He offered 1500/- Rs. to the Peon and bid 'good bye' to him. Joseph informed him that for further follow-ups also Kiran would have to depend on him. The peon had given his mobile number to him for further contact. Kiran retuned home with a peace of mind at least for one day.

When he reached his home a 'registered letter' was waiting for him. It indicated that 'he was suspended from the service with an immediate effect' from May 20th onwards because of lack of integrity, disobedience, and irresponsible attitude towards the institute and his duties and responsibilities. The letter indicates that an organisation requires 'more integrity than PhD degree.'

Discussion Questions

1. Discuss how organisational hierarchy affects the functional deliverables?
2. Discuss the organisational structure of universities that affect the satisfaction of stakeholders?

3. How far corruption and nepotism affect university administration?
4. To what extend the departmentation and centralization affect effective university administration?
5. Discuss the motivational factors of university employees?
6. Discuss the role of training and development programmes required for university employees in their performance improvement?
7. How we can incorporate effective performance appraisal system to university administrative system that contributes to employees functional and responsibility orientation?
8. Develop a plan of action that make university administrative system students centric and create credibility to the deliverables?